# A SOURCEBOOK FOR SUBSTITUTES and other teachers

## miriam k. Freedman & teri Perl

▲ **ADDISON-WESLEY PUBLISHING COMPANY**

Menlo Park, California ● Reading, Massachusetts ● London ● Don Mills, Ontario

## ABOUT THE AUTHORS:

MIRIAM K. FREEDMAN has been a grade 1-12 substitute teacher in Boston, Cambridge, and Long Island for the past few years. She has taught elementary reading in Trenton, New Jersey; social studies in Berkeley, California, and Port Jefferson, New York; and junior high school in Fairfield, California. Presently, she is teaching an early childhood nature course at the Setauket, New York, Environmental Center, and is organizing workshops for substitute teachers. Miriam lives in Stony Brook, New York, with her husband, Dan, a theoretical physicist, and her daughter.

TERI PERL has done secondary substitute teaching in the California school districts of Palo Alto, Sequoia Union, and Mountain View. Presently, she is serving as math consultant for an elementary demonstration school in Palo Alto and is teaching elementary methods courses in mathematics education at California State University Extension, San Jose. She has published articles on mathematics in various journals, and now is developing activity cards and teachers' materials for a new manipulative program in mathematics. Teri lives in Palo Alto with her husband, Martin, an experimental physicist, and her four children.

This book is in the **ADDISON-WESLEY INNOVATIVE SERIES**

*Library of Congress Catalog Card Number* 73–15930
ISBN 0-201-05786-7

11 12 13 14 15 - ML - 95 94 93

# PREFACE

It's dawn and the telephone is ringing. Suddenly we are in front of a new class. There are no lesson plans, or we can't find them, or the ones on the desk are unusable. The class is getting noisy. This is the start of a day that often seems endlessly long and chaotic.

It is because of such days that we started arriving at school prepared with appropriate games and activities.

We used them, and the students enjoyed them. Days went faster. And, best of all, the students were learning!

As one boy with a disastrous reputation spurted, "Usually we run out of the room—but you had a good game, so we were good!"

Soon we found we had assembled a large and interesting collection of materials which worked well and which we wanted to share. Our goal in writing this book has been to change the image of "a day with a substitute" from negative to positive. We will consider such a day well spent when a student can leave school knowing that he has learned something new.

# CONTENTS

*See Also:*
Braille
ESP—Fact or Fantasy?
Family Tree—Root it Out!
Fingerprints
Flow Diagrams
Four-Color Problem
French Culture
Game of 26
Invention or Discovery
Morse Code
Phrenology
Space
Spanish Culture
Ye Olde Word Factory

*Extras*

For All Subjects (requiring some
preparation and outside materials)

# INTRODUCTION

This book is a collection of tested materials which can enrich the standard curriculum when used by substitute teachers as well as regular teachers. Using these materials, the substitute teacher is ideally suited to make a significant contribution to the educational experience.

*How?* The substitute can:

**Provide Variety.** Substitutes offer a break from routine—a new face, a new approach, and new materials.

**Provide Enrichment Materials.** Substitutes can provide students with an opportunity to explore subject areas that may be extremely interesting and important but that are excluded from the regular curriculum by time pressures.

**Provide Learning for the Fun of It.** Substitutes can give students an opportunity to learn something for which they will not ''be held responsible.'' The substitute must come equipped with materials that bring their own incentives and rewards.

**Establish an Environment for Student Success.** We now know that student achievement is affected by teacher expectation. A day with a substitute can offer students a chance to break free from negative self-fulfilling prophecies. The substitute teacher, simply by being a new influence in the classroom, may help enlarge the number of students who experience success in the class. Even a single day with the substitute may have important and surprising consequences.

**Be a Resource Person.** The substitute comes into the classroom with many skills, talents, and interests —from cooking to football to computers to auto tinkering. By harnessing his skills, he becomes an important resource person.

**Benefit the Regular Teacher.** If certain activities prove popular and successful, the students may bring them to the attention of the regular teacher. Thus, the standard curriculum will be enriched.

These activities bring the substitute a varied collection of classroom materials—puzzles, games, discoveries. These materials are arranged according to academic subjects: English, foreign languages, mathematics, science, and social studies. Activities that are applicable to more than one subject are so designated.

Activities that can be used by students working alone, in groups or teams, or as entire classes, are so coded. Whenever possible, we have designed or adapted our activities for group and team play. In our experience as substitutes, we have used this format to great advantage. Students love to play games. Team games foster cooperation within the team and competition among teams. Such games create a supportive atmosphere and remove the burden of poor ability or losing from individual students. Instead, students share their abilities. Because the substitute does not know the students well, this sharing of skills opens the activity to broad student participation. If, however, you want individual students to work alone, you may use most of these activities in this way, too. Many activities are coded for use by students working alone as well as in groups.

Although this book contains a wide range of activities at many levels of difficulty, no attempt is made to code these activities according to difficulty. The backgrounds of the teachers and students using this book will be too varied for such a code to be useful. Activities which seem difficult to some will doubtless seem simple to others. In general, the easiest activities to handle are those based on a ditto that can be handed to the students as they enter the room. The most difficult units to use are those that require the teacher to lead a discussion. The games, though requiring more skillful class management than a handout, are generally popular, and work well.

You will note that very few of our activities require that the students have specific prior knowledge. In our activities, we do not seek to reward information retention (Who wrote *Moby Dick?* What is the capital of Kenya?). Rather, we seek to encourage analytical thinking. When specific answers are required, as in *Family Tree, Braille, Africa Out of Context,* and so on, the answers are usually built into the activity because methods for deriving them are presented. Our hope is to change the image of the teacher as the person with the answer sheet and to open the class to an active learning atmosphere for all—including the teacher! Share the answer sheet!

Our goal in writing this book has been to change the image of a "day with a substitute" from negative to positive. We shall consider such a day well spent if a student leaves school knowing he has learned something new.

## Special Features

**Hints for Success.** From our own teaching experience, we offer practical suggestions for using our materials in the classroom.

**Educational Objectives.** This section is an itemized listing of educational objectives for each activity.

**Classification.** Each activity has been classified by subject, student grouping, and format of materials to help the substitute gather his material quickly and efficiently:

| Subject | Student Groupings | Format |
|---|---|---|
| All subjects | Class as a whole | Dittos |
| English | Groups or teams | Dittos*—special case |
| French | Individuals | |
| Spanish | | |
| Mathematics | | Blackboard |
| Science | | Other |
| Social Studies | | Quickies |

**Subject.** Because many substitutes are asked to teach subjects outside their specialty, activities classified for all subjects can be very helpful. They are extremely flexible. Experiment with them in all classes!

Each activity designed for use in specific subject areas is coded according to the most obvious subject area and according to other subjects appropriate for that activity. For example, a word game may be listed in the English section, but it may also be used equally well in foreign language classes. Activities are also cross-referenced in the Table of Contents. Be flexible! Use activities wherever they seem appropriate.

**Student Groupings.** Class— These activities usually involve group discovery experiences in which class and teacher work together.

Groups or teams— These activities lend themselves to the game format. The suitable number of groups per activity is usually given with the activity. However, use your own judgment. Be flexible! Notice that many activities may be used with more than one type of grouping (individuals and groups, or individuals and classes, or three teams or five teams, and so on). Experiment!

Individuals— These activities may be used by students working alone. The teacher is required to give little or no explanation and guidance. If students seem to have trouble getting started or if they have difficulty later on, perhaps let them work quietly in pairs.

**Format of Materials.** Dittos— Activities to be dittoed are presented in ready-to-use form. The teacher simply has to run them off before class, usually making one copy per individual or team.

Dittos*—Special cases— These activities may be used without a ditto if it is inconvenient to prepare one. Plan your time so you have a few minutes to write the necessary information on the blackboard. Or you may use an overhead projector to display the information necessary to work on the activity. In a few activities, although the ditto is essential for students to do the puzzle part of these activities, there are interesting parts that can be done without a ditto.

Blackboard— These activities require only a blackboard or an overhead or opaque projector.

Quickies— These activities may be used either for an entire period or for only part of one. If, for example, you must use lesson plans, you may fit the quickies into the last five to fifteen minutes of the period. They are easy to organize and will help make the period special. If you use them for the entire period, you may use more than one round or set.

Other— These activities involve materials other than dittos, blackboard, or paper and pencil. Required materials are clearly specified.

# HINTS FOR SUCCESS

## Hints in General

**1. Learn school procedure.** First thing in the morning, find out school procedure related to attendance, building routine, bell signals, lunch, discipline, and whatever else is relevant. *Follow the procedure.* Remember, you are working within a specific environment. If you have a free period, find out more about the environment by talking with teachers over coffee or by walking around and peeking into classrooms. If you have disruptive students in your classes, follow the school procedure related to discipline. Remember, too, it is best to deal with disruptive behavior early, before it escalates.

**2. Start class immediately.** Some students will, as soon as they walk into the room and see the substitute, decide this is the time to do all the goofing off they have been saving for this special day. Don't give them a chance to disrupt. Give them the dittos or rules of the game as they walk into the room. Get them started before they know what hit them! If the material is intriguing and worthwhile, students will usually settle down and have a good period. After the activity is begun, you may walk around, learn some names, and talk about the activity.

One day this method worked especially well. I was asked to substitute in a tough junior high school in central Boston. The teacher hadn't left lesson plans. What to do? As the students sauntered in, I handed out the *Hidden Black Leaders* puzzle. Of course, some students refused to take a sheet. I didn't insist. The puzzle was particularly well suited to be handed out immediately because the rules are self-explanatory. To my great joy (and relief!), the students loved the puzzle. There was a pleasant hum of work. After a while, most of the students who had at first refused the ditto asked for copies. We kept a running score on the board. Great

period! When it was almost over, I tried to collect the puzzles, but about half of the students refused to give them up—they wanted to finish them later. Sure enough, at the end of the day, several came in to show me what they had accomplished!

With other kinds of classes—those in which students are not tense and rowdy—it may be worthwhile to learn names and get acquainted at the very beginning of the period. Procedures for accomplishing this are given below. Also, with this type of class, you may wish to provide motivation for playing the game. (See "Hints for Using the Materials" below.)

**3. Learn names.** People appreciate being recognized as individuals. Taking five to ten minutes out of a period to learn names is time well spent (especially if you will see the class more than one period). If you remember names easily, walk around, ask names, and repeat them. Let the students watch *you* learn. If you are poor at this, you might have students write their names on a folded piece of paper that will be clearly visible to you when placed on the desk or table. Take a few minutes to walk around, read off the names, and check on pronunciation. This is an excellent way to relate to students as individuals! Of course, you will write your own name on the board and pronounce it for the class.

**4. Switch roles.** Should you find yourself with a lesson plan you know nothing about, try switching roles with the students. Let the students explain the lesson to *you.* If this is to be successful, you must let yourself be taught by the students, as well as be genuinely interested in the topic at hand. For their part, the students will have to work at organizing and presenting their materials in a clear and meaningful way—certainly, a valuable learning experience.

**5. Be sensitive to mood.** The successful substitute is sensitive to the mood of the class (and the school and community). If you are in class on a day when a major news story breaks or a local issue is being discussed, you may have difficulty in diverting students' attention away from the story or issue. Don't even try! The successful substitute should be prepared to exploit the educational potential of student involvement. (Furthermore, the class may find it refreshing to discuss current topics with someone other than their regular teacher. It may give them additional freedom to express themselves.) You may take advantage of current events in several ways. The obvious way is to have students talk about the situation. Set ground rules (Raise hands to speak; one person speaks at a time; and so on). If you do not wish to lead the discussion, you or the class may choose a student to do this. Another way of involving students in current events is to have them write letters to officials, if appropriate. Letter writing often gives students a greater sense of accomplishment than does merely talking.

## Hints for Using the Materials

**1. Be enthusiastic.** It is important that you, the substitute, introduce the activity you have chosen with enthusiasm. Phrases like "Here is a puzzle," "Let's play a game," "Have you heard of . . ." usually work well.

**2. Motivate your students.** One of many approaches to motivating students is to *relate to them as a person.* Students are often interested in the substitute as a person. You might tell them something about yourself that relates to the activity you have selected. For example, if you have traveled, you might mention places referred to in geography games. If you know a blind person, the activity on Braille can come alive. If you watch TV, you can relate your viewing experience to any number of activities. Another approach to motivation is to give students *a pretest and a posttest.* Before

a game begins, you might ask students to share any information they may have in the area of the game to be played. Encourage them to spill answers and ideas. These may be written on the blackboard. Then tell them that after the game is played, they will have another opportunity to share their information. Students often find they know much more the second time around. They are thrilled to know they have learned something and enjoyed it at that! This method has been very effective with *Space Games, Hidden Black Leaders, Bingo, Africa Out of Context,* and so on. Whether or not you use the pretest and posttest method, help students understand that they have learned something. The strongest motivation is in the *play-and-learn quality* of the activities. Puzzles provide added motivation in a learning situation—the desire to win or finish in addition to the desire to learn.

Once there was a fire drill—just as the class was working on one of the dittoed puzzles. After the initial cheer that often accompanies this welcomed break from routine, students filed out of class . . . *with their papers.* They worked on them outside! When the drill was over, I was the last one back in the room. The room was quiet and all were working hard.

**3. Keep the activity moving.** Don't hesitate to give answers or hints that will keep the activity moving along and the students feeling cheerful and successful. Encourage students to work together when this will generate success.

**4. Involve students who are not interested.** If there are students in the class who are not interested in the game or activity and are reluctant to participate, try to find something they can do in relation to the activity. Such students often make eager scorekeepers. Keeping a running score on the blackboard adds competition and excitement to any game or activity. (See Hint 5, which follows.) Your apathetic student may ask to join the game. If this happens, find yourself a new scorekeeper and carry on. Should a student refuse to become involved at all, don't force the issue. Let him observe quietly. He may learn merely by being in a stimulating atmosphere. So long as he does not disturb the class, all is well. If he does, follow the disciplinary policy of the school.

**5. Keep a running score.** Scorekeeping is useful not only during a game; it may also motivate individual students working alone. For example, we have kept running scores while doing *Hidden Words* and *Letter Slots*. As students reach specific goals, such as finding a given number of hidden words or completing a given number of hidden words or completing a given number of sets of material, a scorekeeper writes the names on the board. As goals are reached, new ones are set; names previously written on the board may be erased and new names put up. There are many ways of scorekeeping. Experiment with different ones, and find which way works best for you.

**6. Go to the students.** When students are eager to show you their progress, go to the students' desks to take stock rather than having them come to your desk. A great deal of classroom confusion may be avoided if you do this.

**7. Encourage student direction.** Whenever possible, encourage students to direct their own games and puzzles. This gives them good practice and keeps you, the teacher, from talking too much. Furthermore, it maintains class routine because students are more familiar with their routine than is the substitute.

**8. Be flexible.** You may find that after a while you have accumulated a great many dittoed materials. Be flexible. You might have different students, either individually or in small groups, working on different dittos at the same time. Some will ask to take dittos home to try on their parents or siblings. Let them!

**9. Use lesson plans plus.** You should try to squeeze a game into each period, even if the regular teacher has left usable lesson plans. Those games that can be played rapidly are called Quickies. Even a quick game with a substitute will make the period a bit special.

**10. Select teams.** There are several ways to select teams. If two teams are needed, you may team the boys against the girls, have the class count off alternately ("one-two, one-two, . . . ."), divide the class between the right and left sides of the room (perhaps calling one team "the windows," and the other "the doors"), divide them by rows, or so on. If more than two teams are needed, you may count off by however many you need, divide the class by rows, or simply select students at random. It is best not to select captains who then choose teams because this is time-consuming and often leads to hurt feelings. Once teams are chosen, students may select their captains, if necessary.

**11. Choose activities appropriate to the time you have.** Some units in this book are fairly long. In addition to the basic activity, they include discussion questions and suggestions for further exploration. To cover all these materials would clearly require more than one class period. These units may be especially useful if you know you are going to be in a class for more than one day. Remember, however, that these units have been designed with natural breaking points and can easily be tailored to fit one class period.

**Final Note to the Substitute**

After reading these hints, you may feel that some are contradictory. For example, you cannot hand out dittos as students are walking into the room and also start the game off with a pretest. You will have to use your intuition in deciding what to do when.

Teaching demands flexibility, and substitute teaching demands flexibility *plus*.

# EDUCATIONAL OBJECTIVES

## All Subjects

1. *Bingo*
2. *Categories*
3. *Endless Chain of Anything and Everything . . .*
4. *Team Quiz*
5. *Tic-Tac-Toe*
6. *Words in a Word*
7. *WPM (Words Per Minute)*

*Quickies:* To give the teacher an attractive game format for review and drill in all subjects; particularly flexible—usable for long or short periods of time; a core collection — handy, reusable, fun!

8. *Informal Polling:* To design polls, sample opinion, and tabulate results
9. *Treasured Passage Hunt:* To learn the value of tables of contents, indices, and memory as tools for the efficient location of information

## English

1. *Add-a-Letter*
2. *Boxes*
3. *Letter Slots*
4. *Magic Word Squares*
5. *English Quickies:*

To develop agility in the use of letters and words; to reinforce spelling and vocabulary skills. Also, to explore how rumors spread

6. *Braille:* To learn and work with Braille, using it both as a code and as an introduction to the subculture of the blind
7. *Family Tree—Root it out!* To learn and to explore the system of family relationships; a unit in genealogy
8. *Game of 26:* To improve the skills of observation, memory, and categorization
9. *Memory Dial:* To introduce and practice the use of a classic memory device
10. *Morse Code:* To learn and work with Morse Code; to explore its usage, past and present

11. *Say What You Mean and Mean What You Say!* To develop precision in the use of language
12. *Ye Olde Word Factory:* To help students discover the meaning of new words by constructing them from prefixes, suffixes, and roots

## Foreign Language

1. *French Add-a-Letter*
2. *Spanish Add-a-Letter*
3. *French Letter Slots*
4. *Spanish Letter Slots*
5. *Les Aliments*
6. *Las Comidas*

To build vocabulary; to develop agility in the use of foreign words

7. *The Living Room*
   *Le Salon*
   *La Sala*
8. *Le Corps; El Cuerpo*

To build vocabulary; to focus on similarities among languages

9. *French Culture*
10. *Spanish Culture*

To expand acquaintance with French and Spanish culture and geography

## Math

1. *Dicey Tic Tac Toe:* To develop skill using number pairs
2. *Fibonacci Sequence:* To learn to generate a number sequence which has intrigued mathematicians for centuries
3. *Flow Diagrams:* To learn to diagram a problem in clear logical sequence; a necessary first step in computer programming
4. *Forest Fire Fighters:* To practice plotting number pairs in a game setting
5. *Four-color Problem:* To give students experience exploring a famous unsolved problem in mathematics; to practice locating countries on a map.
6. *Kard Kapers:* To develop flexibility in the use of numbers and mathematical operations

7. *Lines to Curves:* To highlight the relationship between lines and curves by generating attractive geometric designs; to explore how these curves change under different variables

8. *Math Quickies:* To provide a quick look at a different method of multiplication, a problem in topology, and a geometric problem which generates an algebraic function

9. *Nim Type Games:* To sharpen development of game strategy skills using simple rules and arithmetic

10. *Number Games and Puzzles:* To play with numbers. How many ways can you name "X"?

11. *Palindromic Numbers:* To generate addition practice in a fresh context by using palindromes

12. *Paths, Routes, and Circuits:* In a puzzle context, to introduce students to some interesting theorems in topology

13. *Pictographs I* } To practice plotting
    *Pictographs II* } number pairs.

14. *Polyominoes:* To explore ways in which geometric shapes can be combined; an exercise in combinatorial geometry

15. *Graph Paper:* To provide graph paper

## Science

1. *Compare the Pair!* To practice organizing data gathered from observation

2. *E.S.P.—Fact or Fantasy?* To conduct a probability experiment using the methodology of a controversial scientific field, parapsychology

3. *Experiment With Pulse, Breath, Hands, Eyes:* To make observations and conclusions based on experiments

4. *Explore Learning:* To gain insight into some mechanisms of learning

5. *Fingeristics:* To give students practice in observation and collection of data using the measure of their fingers as the data

6. *Fingerprints:* To learn the code and methodology of fingerprint classification and to use these skills to identify individuals by their fingerprints

7. *Hidden Elements:* To learn the names of specific chemical elements in a puzzle format which requires efficient scanning techniques

8. *Invention or Discovery?* To focus on the difference between invention and discovery; to familiarize students with inventors and discoverers and their achievements through a matching puzzle, game, and discussion questions

9. *Now You See It, Now You Don't:* To have students discover certain physiological properties about themselves through simple experiments and to practice organizing data

10. *Phrenology:* To help students develop a critical approach to new sciences by exploring an example of one, now discredited, which enjoyed a respectable role in the past

11. *Physics Fun:* To explore some fundamental laws of physics

12. *Space Games:* To focus on some of the terminology used in the exploration of space; to look at the possible value of this exploration to different branches of science

13. *The World is a Freshwater Pond:* To begin to develop an understanding of the interrelationships that form an ecological system

## Social Studies

1. *Africa Out of Context:* To discover the geography of African countries through their shapes

2. *Anthro Homes:* Using pictures of artifacts from various cultures to draw valid conclusions about these cultures

3. *Cities Go, Cities Grow:* To explore the change in rank between major U.S. cities within a given interval of time

4. *Europe Out of Context:* To discover the geography of European countries through their shapes

5. *Free Us! We're Sentenced:* To develop skill in reducing sentences and words to component letters, and regrouping these letters into the names of states, Presidents, and countries; a kind of code reading

6. *Games and Fields:* To sharpen skills of observation and deduction in a context of popular sports; to explore questions about these sports in general

7. *Hidden Black Leaders:* To familiarize students with the names of prominent black people in a puzzle which requires efficient scanning techniques

8. *Hidden States:* To reinforce recognition and spelling of the states in a puzzle which requires efficient scanning techniques

9. *Proceed with Caution:* To explore existing road signs, their characteristic shapes; to introduce students to international road sign systems and to explore their advantages and disadvantages

10. *Scrambled Cities U.S.A.:* A scrambled word game involving U.S. cities and their locations

11. *Stop, You're Under Arrest:* To study the structure of the criminal judicial procedure

12. *U.S.A. Out of Context:* To discover the geography of the United States through the shapes of the states

**Extras for All Subjects**

1. *Standardized Tests Workshop:* To provide practice in handling standardized tests

2. *Substitute's Bag of Skills, Talents, and Interests:* To focus attention on the use of the substitute's own talents and interests as sources for classroom learning

# BINGO!

**Object:** To cover five cells in a row (horizontally, vertically, or diagonally) on a 5 by 5 grid.

**Materials:** Paper and pencil.

**Preparation:** Have students draw a large 5 by 5 grid on their papers. Have them put an *X* in the middle square or free space. Also have small pieces of paper cut or torn (by you ahead of time or by the students in class) to cover individual squares on the bingo board as words are called. Choose the game topic or category. There are numerous categories you might choose. In English classes, you might use authors' names, synonyms or antonyms, three-syllable words, words with letter pairs, etc. In foreign languages, you might use names of foods, parts of the body, verbs, or French authors. In math, possibilities include square numbers, prime numbers, multiples. In social studies, possible topics include presidents, countries, states, famous people, or rivers. In science, use the elements, plants, minerals, etc.

The class as a whole should think of the twenty-four items needed to fill the twenty-four cells on the board. (Recall that the middle square is free.) Finding twenty-four items in a particular category may be the most educational aspect of the game. If it is impossible for the class to think of twenty-four items in a reasonable amount of time, move on to another category or let the students write some items twice. As items are decided, they are written three times: on the board, so all students see the correct spelling; on the students' own grids in random order, so all papers look different; and on small slips of paper to be used later for the drawing.

**The play:** The teacher or a student draws a slip of paper and reads off an item. As each item is read, students cover that item on their papers. When a student has covered five in a row, he calls "Bingo!" Then he reads off all his items. If each item has been called off, he is the winner and may be the next caller. The game may continue for as many rounds as you like.

**Variations:** Note that most categories have sister categories; that is, they can be called off in different ways. To heighten the value of the game in a foreign language, for example, instead of calling a food or part of the body in French, call off the translation in English. Let the students figure out what to cover on their papers. In social studies, instead of calling the states shown on the playing grids, call the state capitals. If it is too hard for the student caller to think of sister categories, you may prepare a list for him. Or he may call off the items he knows best first, instead of picking slips at random, and hope that someone will call "Bingo" before he has run into items he cannot convert into sister categories.

Another variation is to have students exchange playing grids for some rounds.

# CATEGORIES

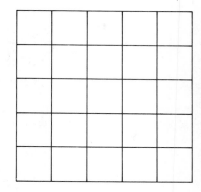

**Object:** To fill a 5 by 5 grid with words in a particular category.

**Materials:** Paper and pencil.

**Student groupings:** If you use groups, they should be made up of two to five members each.

**Preparation:** All students or groups draw a 5 by 5 grid on their papers. Each of the twenty-five cells should be large enough to contain a word.

**The play:** The class agrees on five categories within a given subject area and writes each one in a slot at the left-hand side of the grid. Then five letters (or a five-letter word) are agreed upon. These letters are written at the top of the five columns. (See the examples below.) Within a given time period, each student or team attempts to fill in each cell in the grid with an item appropriate to that cell's category and given letter.

**Examples:**

| In science: | R | S | C | F | E |
|---|---|---|---|---|---|
| Flowers | rose | sunflower | clover | | |
| Inventors | | | | Fermi | Edison |
| Symbols of elements | | S | C | Fe | |
| Machines | | shovel | | | elevator |
| Parts of body | retina | skin | chest | face | eye |

| In French: | C | S | A | D | M |
|---|---|---|---|---|---|
| Food | | Sucre | | | |
| Parts of the body | Coeur | | | | main |
| Cities | Caen | | Amiens | Dijon | Marseilles |
| Verbs | | Sortir | Aller | Dormir | |
| Famous people of France | Camus | Sartre | | DeGaulle | |

| In math: | G | R | A | P | H |
|---|---|---|---|---|---|
| Geometry terms | | radius | angle | | height |
| Math terms (no geometry) | graph | remainder | answer | | |
| Numbers | | | | | |
| Famous Mathematicians | | | Abel | Pythagoras | |
| Occupations using math | | | accountant | painter | |

**Scoring:** This may be the most important educational aspect of the game. Ask each student or team to give its letter and category combinations. This may take a long time, but it's worth it. It's fun—and informative—for the class to hear what others have come up with. As you go over items, ask each student or team to keep its own score: one point for each correct answer, three points for each correct answer that no one else had, five points for each correct answer in a cell that no one else could fill.

**Note:** Students may play several rounds with different categories and/or different letter combinations.

# Endless Chain Of Anything And Everything

Here's an excellent quickie. It is easy to explain, and no materials are needed. And, it's lots of fun.

**KANSAS CITY ➡**
**NEWPORT ➡**
**YOUNGSTOWN**
**NEWTON**

**Object:** To continue the chain as long as possible.

**Materials:** None

**Student groupings:** Two or more teams.

**The play:** You, the teacher, and/or the class choose a category. One team starts by giving a word within that category. The next team notes the *last letter* of the word given and must give a word beginning with that letter. Students within teams take turns answering for their team. Teams continue to take turns until one team cannot continue the chain. Then, a new category is chosen and a new chain is begun. (See examples below.)

**Examples:** The category is authors. The chain may proceed from Hawthorne to Eliot to Twain to Norris to Shakespeare to Emerson. . .

The category is mathematical terms. The game proceeds from square to ellipse to equation to nine to equal to linear to rectangle. . .

The category is countries. The game proceeds from United States to Sweden to Norway to Yugoslavia to Albania to Australia. . .

**Scoring:** The team that fails to continue the chain forfeits a point to the other team(s). The team with the most points at the end of the game wins.

**Note:** Within a chain, no word may be repeated.

# Informal Polling

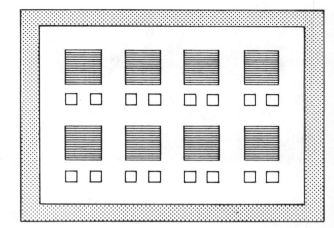

This may be used when the substitute gives the class a study period. Students who have no work to do may enjoy this poll-taking experience.

**Object:** To give students an opportunity to design polls, obtain a sampling of opinions, and tabulate poll results.

**Materials:** Paper and pencil.

**Student groupings:** Individuals or small groups. This activity is best done by only part of a class.

**Preparation:** Have the student(s) who will make the poll write a questionnaire of about five items. The items should elicit a wide range of responses; that is, they should be interesting to answer. Have the students avoid questions directed against specific people. (a fellow student, a regular teacher, the local policeman). Be sure that you, the teacher, approve the questions before they are used.

**Examples:** Questions will usually be of four types:

1. Opinion questions: Should there be a 10:00 P.M. curfew for people our age? Who will you vote for in the next election? What is the biggest environmental problem our town faces?

2. Information questions: Who is the president of the U.S.? vice-president? governor of the state? mayor? senators? principal of the school? Have students write down their answers. Then count the numbers right. Which is known by most? Why?

   How many students walked outside less than fifteen minutes today? more than 15 minutes?

   How many students brought lunch today? How many brought potato chips? soda? sandwich? fruit? candy?

   How many students, in the last three days, talked to an older person (other than their parents or teachers)? to a little child (other than their brothers or sisters)?

How many students read a newspaper? what section? comics? news? sports? stocks? TV? features? women's page? other?

How many watched TV last night? How long? one hour or less? one to two hours? two to three hours? longer?

How many students, in the last week, used the public library? park? museum? pool or beach? gym? playground?

3. Value-ranked questions: Which would you rather be: (a) rich; (b) famous; (c) well liked?

4. Open-ended questions: My favorite singing group is _____; School is _____.

All questions should be designed to elicit definite, though different responses, and should include an "I don't know" or "No opinion" option.

**Procedure:** The poll may be taken in one of two ways:

1. Have the student(s) go around the room polling everyone in the class. Answers may be collected in one group or separated into groups. In other words, the answers of boys may be differentiated from those of girls, the answers of participants in school athletics from those of nonparticipants, and so on.

2. Have the student(s) conduct a secret ballot. The polltaker reads off each question to all the students. Students write down their opinions and hand them in.

After all students have been questioned, the results should be tabulated. In math classes this can be done in several elaborate ways, with results shown in fractions, averages, or percentages. The polltaker(s) should show the figures and summarize the results in some meaningful way (by graphs, charts, tables). The students should also be asked to think about the types of questions that elicited the best or most interesting responses.

# TEAM QUIZ

This game is particularly useful in helping a class review materials.

**Object:** To guess the item chosen by an opposing team.

**Materials:** None.

**Student groupings:** Teams of five to ten members each.

**The play:** The students together agree on a broad category of objects, persons, places, or events. Preferably, the category should be related to their study. Broad categories include words in a foreign language, words related to American history, something in the room, etc. Without letting other teams know its decision, each team then selects an object within the category. The harder, the better! Each team also selects a representative.

At your signal, each representative moves to another team, which questions him about his team's item. The questioning team tries to find out which item the representative's team's has chosen. All questions must be answerable with a yes, a no, or an "I don't know."

The first team to guess a representative's item wins, and the round is over. All representatives go back to their own teams. A new item, and a new representative are chosen. Play as many rounds as you wish.

**Scoring:** Each time a team guesses an item, it scores a point. The team with the most points at the end of the game wins.

**Variations:** This activity may cause noise and confusion because several groups are questioning students simultaneously. To reduce noise, you may amend the rules by counting the number of questions a group has to ask to obtain the answer. The competition is thus changed from a race against time to a race for the least number of questions. The whole class may listen as each group proceeds. The low score wins.

# Tic Tac Toe

**Object:** To cover three cells in a row, vertically, diagonally, or horizontally.

**Materials:** Paper and pencil or chalk and blackboard.

**Student groupings:** Divide the class into two teams.

**Preparation:** A tic-tac-toe grid is drawn on the blackboard or on paper. You and/or the class decide on the topic for the tic-tac-toe round of games. You write down items within that topic (one in each cell). Several game rounds using these items are possible. (See the examples.)

**The play:** Members of teams take turns choosing a cell to answer. If the answer is correct, their team gets a mark for that cell. You may use X and O for the two teams. The team that first gets three marks in a row wins. Another round of questions and answers can be played with the same nine items, or a new set may be used. This game can be played as long as students *are* interested, seem to be learning from it, and you have time.

**Examples:** Here are some social studies grids:

**Countries**

| U.S. | France | India |
|------|--------|-------|
| Ghana | Great Britain | Brazil |
| Iraq | Hungary | U.S.S.R. |

**Some Rounds:**

1. Give capitals.
2. Give leader's name.
3. Give continents.
4. Name a river, city, or famous person.

**President's initials**

| G.C. | U.S.G. | J.A. |
|------|--------|------|
| G.W. | R.M.N. | J.F.K. |
| A.L. | W.W. | T.J. |

**Some rounds:**

1. Give president's name.
2. Name president who preceded (succeeded) him.
3. Give president's political party.

Here are some math grids:

| 5 | 7 | 9 |
|----|----|----|
| 13 | 15 | 12 |
| 1 | 4 | 3 |

This is a simple game. The grid may look like this. For each game using this grid, choose a particular function. For example, a very easy one might be $x + c$. Here, the $c$'s are the values in the cells. For one game pick a single value of $x$. Decide, for example, that $x = 5$. At his turn, each student must give the value of the cell he is trying to win. If $x = 5$, then:

| $5 + 5$ | $7 + 5$ | $9 + 5$ |
|---------|---------|---------|
| $13 + 5$ | $15 + 5$ | $12 + 5$ |
| $1 + 5$ | $4 + 5$ | $3 + 5$ |

| 10 | 12 | 14 |
|----|----|----|
| 18 | 20 | 17 |
| 6 | 9 | 8 |

Here is a more complicated math grid.

| $4x - 8$ | $x^2 + 2$ | $3x + 5$ |
|----------|-----------|----------|
| $2x$ | $x^2$ | $6x - 7$ |
| $x^2 - 5$ | $x + 2x$ | $x^3$ |

For example, if in round one, $x = 3$, then

| $(4 \cdot 3) - 8$ | $(3 \cdot 3) + 2$ | $(3 \cdot 3) + 5$ |
|-------------------|-------------------|-------------------|
| $2 \cdot 3$ | $3 \cdot 3$ | $(6 \cdot 3) - 7$ |
| $(3 \cdot 3) - 5$ | $3 + (2 \cdot 3)$ | $3 \cdot 3 \cdot 3$ |

| 4 | 11 | 14 |
|----|----|----|
| 6 | 9 | 11 |
| 4 | 9 | 27 |

21

You might decide that the function is $c$ times $x$. If, for example, $x = 3$, then

| 5 | 7 | 9 |
|---|---|---|
| 13 | 15 | 12 |
| 1 | 4 | 3 |

| 5 x 3 | 7 x 3 | 9 x 3 |
|---|---|---|
| 13 x 3 | 15 x 3 | 12 x 3 |
| 1 x 3 | 4 x 3 | 3 x 3 |

| 15 | 21 | 27 |
|---|---|---|
| 39 | 45 | 36 |
| 3 | 12 | 9 |

Remember, you may use *one* function for the entire period and continue to change the $x$. For example, if you want to reinforce the meaning of $x^2 = x$ times $x$, you may use $x^2$ as your function for the period. The numbers in the grid are now the values for $x$:

| 5 | 7 | 9 |
|---|---|---|
| 13 | 15 | 12 |
| 1 | 4 | 3 |

| 5 x 5 | 7 x 7 | 9 x 9 |
|---|---|---|
| 13 x 13 | 15 x 15 | 12 x 12 |
| 1 x 1 | 4 x 4 | 3 x 3 |

| 25 | 49 | 81 |
|---|---|---|
| 169 | 225 | 144 |
| 1 | 16 | 9 |

In subsequent games, you may merely change the numbers in the grid, and play using the same function, $x^2$.

**Variations:** The possibilities for tic-tac-toe are amazing—limited only by your ingenuity. Be flexible. Also, encourage the class to think of new games and categories.

# TREASURED PASSAGE HUNT

This provides good practice in using organizational aids in a book and in listening carefully. It's a great quickie!

**Object:** To give students valuable practice in understanding and using a book's organizational aids—title page, table of contents, index, and so on. Also, to give students a quick view or review of an entire book.

**Materials:** All students should have a copy of the same book, probably the class textbook for a particular subject.

**The play:** One student volunteers or is chosen. He chooses a passage from the book to read. He may choose any passage anywhere in the book, including sections not yet studied. He reads the passage aloud to his classmates. The passage should be several sentences long, perhaps a full paragraph. As soon as his classmates hear the reading, they begin to search for this passage, using any method they like: their memory, the table of contents, the index. There are usually clues to help students find the passage—a person's name, a place, a particular problem. Whoever finds the passage first wins and becomes the next reader. The reader may also describe pictures, graphs, paintings, and maps. In math classes, students may read a set of problems or a set of instructions.

By the end of the period, the passages read will usually be shorter and trickier than those read at the beginning. Hopefully, students will also have improved their ability to find passages rapidly. You should act as referee and make certain that passages that are too tricky are not read.

If the same students always find the passages first, you may wish to limit the number of times they can be readers or ask them to select other readers. Or, you may ask the third, fourth, and fifth finder of a particular passage to become the next reader.

# Words in a Word

## A REAL QUICKIE!

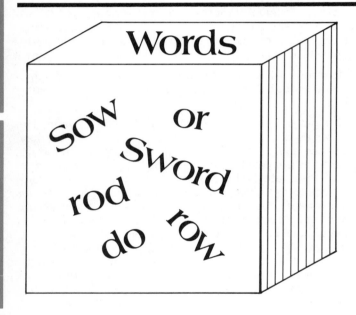

Words

Sow    or
Sword
rod    row
do

**Object:** To form as many words as possible, using the letters of a given word.

**Materials:** Paper and pencil, blackboards and chalk.

**Student groupings:** Individuals or small groups of two or three students each.

**The play:** You write a word on the board. It should be fairly long, like "television," "mathematics," "holidays," etc. In a given time period (like ten minutes), students use the given letter to make up as many words as they can. In each word, letters may be used in any order, but only as often as they appear in the given word. For example, in mathematics, *m* may be used twice, but *s* only once. You may decide that words must have a minimum number of letters, such as three or four letters. As the game proceeds, you should look over papers to see that students are making real words and using correct spelling.

**Scoring:** The person or group with the most words at the end of the time period wins.

**Note:** Several rounds may be played. Words may be limited to a specific subject.

**Example:** Using "television" here is the beginning of a list of possible words:

tile   stone   list   stove   lost   lion
nest   vision   lint   net   ten   etc.

Note here all words have at least three letters.

# WPM
## (Words Per Minute)

**Object:** To give the longest number of words that begin with a given letter within a fixed time interval.

**Materials:** A clock or watch with a second hand, or a timer.

**Student groupings:** Two or more teams.

**Preparation:** You and the class decide on the category or words to be used.

**Examples:** There are numerous possibilities for categories. In English and foreign language classes, use any words, or restrict words to verbs or objects, book titles or authors. In math classes, use any math term, or numbers, or mathematicians. In science, use any science words, names of elements, plants, or planets. In social studies, use any social studies words, names of cities, countries, or famous people.

**The play:** Set a time limit for giving words (say one minute); check the clock, and call off the letter with which words must begin. Then the team whose turn it is calls off as many words as possible beginning with that letter. Words may be called off by an individual team member or by the whole team together (if this doesn't cause too much noise). As words are given, a running score is kept on the board; for example,

After the minute is up, the number of words called is tabulated, and the next team begins with a new letter. Play as many rounds as you like.

The comparative frequency with which different letters are found at the beginning of words in English, French, and Spanish follow. Obviously, teams should be given letters that appear with about the same frequency if the game is to be fair. The frequency with which letters appear at the beginning of words is, from highest to lowest:

**English:** s c p a b m t d r h f e l i g w n o u v k j q y z x

**French:** p c a r s e d m t b f i v g l o n h j q u z k w x y

**Spanish:** c a p d e r t m s b i g f v l h n ch o j z u q ll y k ñ x

**Scoring:** Add the number of words that each team has collected from all the rounds. The highest score wins.

**Note:** In foreign language classes, it is good to have a practice run in English to get into the swing of the game and also to see how hard it is to think of words even in one's own native tongue under time pressure!

| TEAM A | TEAM B |
|--------|--------|
| 卌 卌 <br> 卌 卌 <br> ‖ | 卌 卌 <br> 卌 卌 <br> ‖‖ |

No word is counted more than once, and only one form of a word may be used. For example, if *run* is called, then *ran* or *running* do not count.

# Add-A-Letter

Add a letter to the word at the left to get an example of or a synonym for the word at the right. Letters may sometimes be left in the same order but must usually be rearranged:

Example: Add a letter to PANEL to get a HEAVENLY BODY.

Answer: Planet.

**1.** Add a letter to ENDS to get TAKES CARE OF. _____

**2.** Add a letter to RETAIN to get SURE. _____

**3.** Add a letter to THIS to get SOMETHING TO WEAR. _____

**4.** Add a letter to SEAT to get FLAVOR. _____

**5.** Add a letter to ANTHEM to get A KIND OF GAS. _____

**6.** Add a letter to GRINS ☺ to get QUIT. _____

**7.** Add a letter to STEIN to get QUIET. _____

**8.** Add a letter to POISED to get INCIDENT. _____

**9.** Add a letter to HASTENS to get SHACKS. _____

**10.** Add a letter to HEATERS to get CINEMAS. _____

**11.** Add a letter to BRUTE to get a SERVANT. _____

**12.** Add a letter to REELING to get UNDERGARMENTS. _____

**13.** Add a letter to REVERSING to get KEEPING. _____

**14.** Add a letter to DART to get EXCHANGE. _____

**15.** Add a letter to INFLAME to get a FINE THIN THREAD. _____

**16.** Add a letter to ACHE to get WATERFRONT. _____

**17.** Add a letter to MUCH to get PALS. _____

**18.** Add a letter to BARGAINED to get a KIND OF CLOTH. (pl.) _____

**19.** Add a letter to POET to get a STOREHOUSE. _____

**20.** Add a letter to LATER to get TELL. _____

**21.** Add a letter to FLIRT to get SOMETHING OF LITTLE IMPORTANCE. _____

**22.** Add a letter to LEAST to get a PALE COLOR. _____

**23.** Add a letter to STARVELING to get ETERNAL. _____

**24.** Add a letter to REPENT to get a GIFT. _____

**25.** Add a letter to DISMAY to get VAST NUMBERS. _____

**Answers to Add A Letter**

1. tends
2. certain
3. shirt
4. taste
5. methane
6. resign
7. silent
8. episode
9. shanties
10. theaters
11. butler
12. lingerie
13. preserving
14. trade
15. filament
16. beach
17. chums
18. gabardines
19. depot
20. relate
21. trifle
22. pastel
23. everlasting
24. present
25. myriads

# BOXES I

**Object:** To use the letters given to make horizontal and vertical words in a grid.

**Materials:** Paper and pencil.

**Preparation:** Students draw a 4 by 4 grid on their papers, large enough so a letter can be written in each cell.

**The play:** Here are two versions both of which may be played for as many rounds as you like.

1. Students take turns calling off random letters, one at a time. Or you, as teacher, call off sixteen letters. As soon as a letter is called, all students write it in a cell in their grid. Once written, a letter may *not* be erased. Students try to position their letters in a way that will help them form words. A specific letter may be called more than once—vowels, especially, are called often. Some letters may not be called at all.

2. This version is less subject to chance. You write sixteen letters on the board at one time. In a given time period (five to ten minutes), students are to use these letters to form as many words as possible.

**Scoring:** Words within words do not count, as *then* and *hen*. In this case, the word *then* is counted as a four-letter word. Students should keep track of their scores, giving themselves five points for a four-letter word, three points for a three-letter word, and one point for a two-letter word.

**Example:**

```
P  L  E  H
T  I  M  E
W  E  O  L
R  E  S  P
```
= 13 points

**Variations:** Boxes may be played on a 3 by 3 grid, or a 5 by 5 grid. If a 3 by 3 grid is used, give three points for a three-letter word and one point for a two-letter word. If a 5 by 5 grid is used, give five points for a five-letter word, three points for a four-letter word, and one point for a three-letter word.

# BOXES II

**Object:** To use the numbers given to form true addition sentences in a grid. Number sentences may be vertical, horizontal, or diagonal.

**Materials:** Same as for Boxes I.

**The play:** Again, there are two versions:

1. Students take turns calling any number between 1 and 25. Dice, if available, may be thrown. They add an element of chance. Use four dice to get to a possible 24. As soon as a number is called, all students write it in a cell in their grid. Once written, a number may *not* be erased or moved. Students try to position numbers in a way that will help them form true addition sentences, with the sum of the first three numbers equaling the fourth number on the vertical, horizontal, or diagonal axis.

2. Write sixteen numbers on the board at one time. The numbers should be between 1 and 25, and some numbers may be repeated.

**Scoring:** One point is given for each true addition sentence.

**Examples:**

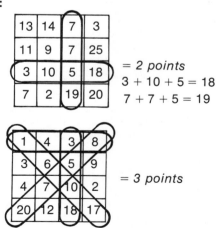

= 2 points
3 + 10 + 5 = 18
7 + 7 + 5 = 19

= 3 points

**Variations:** *Boxes II* may be played on a 3 by 3 grid or a 5 by 5 grid.

# BRAILLE

Today you'll begin to learn how to read and write Braille, the system used by the blind. If this sheet of paper were really Braille, the letters would be punched out, not printed, so the blind could feel them.

Here is the alphabet, some numerals, and other essentials:

The numeral sign placed before a character, makes it a figure, not a letter. Now you're all set!

| 1 | 2 | 3 | 4 | 5 | 6 | 7 | 8 | 9 | 0 |
|---|---|---|---|---|---|---|---|---|---|
| A | B | C | D | E | F | G | H | I | J | K | L | M | N | O |

| P | Q | R | S | T | U | V | W | X | Y | Z | Period | ? | Numeral |

Write your name in Braille:
   ("punch" the points.)

Write your address in Braille:

Now answer these questions—in Braille of course!:

**The Questions in *Braille* Are:**

1. What is your favorite TV show?

2. Do you know a blind person?

3. What is your substitute's name?

4. Where would you like to go on vacation?

**Exploratory Questions**

Have students study the patterns of the Braille dots.

Then discuss these questions in class:

1. Can you find a pattern running consecutively from letter to letter? There is a definite one. For how many letters does it last? When is the pattern repeated (with the addition of the same dot to each letter)? When is it repeated for the second time again, (with the addition of the same dot to the pattern)? *Answers:* The pattern runs for ten letters, then repeats itself for the next ten, then repeats itself for the last five letters (excluding the *W*). Thus, *A* and *K* are the same, except for the addition of the dot in the lower left. And *A, K,* and *U* are the same, except for the addition of the dot in the lower right. Also, *B, L,* and *V* form the same type of trio, etc.

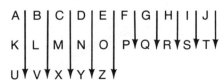

2. Which letter does not fit the pattern? Can you think of why? There is a historical explanation having to do with the language in which Braille was first set down. Answers: The *W* does not fit the pattern. Braille was first set down in French, in which a W is used only rarely. In early Braille, no provision was made for *W*.

3. In each letter or symbol, at least one dot is used from which column? Why do you suppose this is so? In each letter, at least one dot is used from which row? Why do you suppose this is so? *Answers*: In all letters or symbols, at least one dot from the left column appears. In all letters, at least one dot from the top row appears. This is probably done to help the blind person orient his position in relation to the six possible dots per letter.

# ENGLISH QUICKIES
## Challenging, easy to get started, fun!

# Letter Trios and Quadruples

**Object:** To form words using given consonants in specific order.

**Materials:** Paper and pencil. Blackboard is helpful. Let students use books and dictionaries.

**Preparation:** Write the consonant trios and quads on the board.

**Examples:** 1. lkl  2. bsc  3. bst  4. rnm  5. dsl
6. xgl  7. stb  8. nct  9. nkn  10. rth  11. mph
12. ngh  13. ntl  14. nsp  15. stl  16. bstr
17. nstr  18. nchr  19. ndz  20. bscr  21. wkw
22. ndl  23. ncr  24. ngl  25. ntm

**The play:** The students are to form words using the letters given. They do this by adding letters preceding and following the consonant trios and quads. The order may not be changed, and no vowels may be inserted between the given letters. Only one word should be given for each set of consonants. No proper nouns should be counted.

**Scoring:** Scoring is done as a class activity, as each student or team calls off a word for each set of consonants. One point is given for each word. One extra point is given if any student or group is the only one able to make a word from a particular set of consonants.

**Sample answers:** Remember that none of these is the only possible answer.

1. fol*kl*ore
2. a*bsc*ond
3. a*bst*ain
4. gover*nm*ent
5. mu*dsl*ing
6. fox*gl*ove
7. fro*stb*ite
8. fu*nct*ion
9. u*nkn*own
10. ea*rth*en
11. lym*ph*atic
12. gi*ngh*am
13. gau*ntl*et
14. i*nsp*ire
15. li*stl*ess
16. a*bstr*act
17. pi*nstr*ipe
18. sy*nchr*onize
19. e*ndz*one
20. su*bscr*ibe
21. a*wkw*ard
22. ca*ndl*e
23. i*ncr*ement
24. ti*ngl*e
25. oi*ntm*ent

**Variations:** Ask students if any of the sets are acronyms (words or names of organizations formed from the initials of the words in the name.)

If trios and quads seem too difficult for the class, begin by using pairs of letters that seem unusual: for example, ld: gold; dl: seedless; xt: mixture. Later, let them try the trios and quads!

# Word Triangles

**Object:** To form progressively longer words, using the letters given.

**Materials and student groupings:** Same as in previous activity.

**Student groupings:** Individuals or small groups.

**Preparation:** Write the sets of letters on the board, one set at a time. Here are several sets of letters that work well. Numbers in parentheses refer to perfect scores—when there is progression from a one-letter word to a word using all the given letters.

1. ptoslea (28)
2. stelrpas (36)
3. miceponart (55)
4. reserpnigve (66)
5. sssretnip (45)
6. pnaesshr (36)
7. orcdgsrein (55)
8. stlhaemr (36)

**The play:** There are at least three variations for playing *Word Triangles.*

1. Most competitive: Have students take turns, either as team members or as individuals, in calling out one word at a time. Words should go from the shortest to the longest.

2. Have students work out each set of letters alone or in groups. As soon as someone completes a triangle, move on to the next set of letters.

3. Least competitive: Give out all sets of letters at once, and have all students work on them at their desks at their own pace.

**Scoring:** Each letter used in a word is worth 1 point; the highest score wins.

**Example:**   a = 1      rain = 4
                      an = 2      train = 5
                      ran = 3      strain = 6

All together, these words are worth 21 points.

**Note:** You may allow students to form progressively longer words out of *any* of the given letters or restrict them to adding one *new* letter to form each successive word. For example, if the letters were PNCIER, the progression *l, in, ice, rice,* etc. would be possible with the first set of rules, but not with the second, since the *n* is not continued beyond the second word, and in the third word, two new letters, *e* and *c,* are added.

## Sample answers

None of these is the only possible answer.

**1. PTOSLEA**

a
as
sat
past
paste
pastel
apostle

**2. STELRPAS**

a
at
ate
tale
stale
pastel
stapler
staplers

**3. MICEPONART**

a
at
cat
cart
crate
canter
certain
reaction
cremation
importance

**4. RESERPNIGVE**

l
in
gin
grin
rings
singer
serving
severing
reserving
preserving
persevering

**5. SSSRETNIP**

l
in
tin
pint
print
sprint
sprints
spinster
spinsters

**6. PNAESSHR**

a
as
sap
peas
phase
phrase
sharpen
sharpens

**7. ORCDGSREIN**

l
in
din
rind
diner
ringed
grinder
ordering
recording
recordings

**8. STLHAEMR**

a
am
mat
team
steam
stream
hamster
thermals

32

# Gossip

**Object:** To experience how gossip and rumors start and spread.

**Materials:** None.

**Student groupings:** Two groups or teams or class as a whole.

**Preparation:** Write a brief description of an event, such as: ''Mrs. Jones came home, saw the door open and the light on. She knew she had turned it off. She called the police. . .'' or ''Joe saw Matt and Anne at the movies last night. They were whispering to each other. Suddenly she got up and ran out of the theater. . .''

Make two copies.

**The play:** Show the words to the first student in each group. Then take them away. Have him describe the scene in a whisper to his neighbor, the neighbor whispers to his neighbor, and on down the line. When the last student of each group has heard the message, have him tell what he heard. Compare this with the written scene. Discuss how rumors and gossip start and spread. Perhaps try another scene.

# Word Ladders

**Object:** To form either very long or very short words with specified first and last letters.

**Materials and student groupings:** Same as in Letter Trios .

**Preparation:** Take any common English word and write it vertically on the board. Skip some space, and write the same word next to it, vertically, but with the letters reversed. For example,

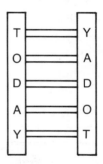

**The play:** Within a given time period (three to five minutes), have students write in words beginning with the first letter shown and ending with the second letter shown. In the preceding examples, the first word might be *toy* or *Thursday*, and the second *omega*. Specify whether words should be as short or as long as possible before starting each set. You may wish to alternate the play between long and short words. Play as many rounds as you like.

**Scoring:** Scoring is done by individual students. Each letter used is worth 1 point. For example, toy = 3, Thursday = 8. The game may be played for either the highest score (when words are supposed to be long), or the lowest (when words are supposed to be short). A penalty of five points should be imposed for any letter pairs left unused. This can be done either by adding or subtracting five points from the total score, depending on whether you are playing for high or low points.

# FAMILY TREE

## Root it Out!

Some family relations get very complicated! See whether you can figure out the ones below! What relation to *you* is

1. your first cousin's uncle's mother? _____

2. your aunt's mother's father's wife? _____

3. your sister's father's stepson's mother? _____

4. Your father's father's daughter's daughter? _____

5. your sister-in-law's father-in-law's grandson? _____

6. your mother's nephew's daughter's son? _____

7. your father's uncle's brother's wife? _____

8. your uncle's father's only grandchild? _____

9. your brother-in-law's wife's grandfather's wife? _____

10. your brother's son's sister's mother? _____

11. your father's father's wife's daughter-in-law? _____

12. your mother's son's daughter's only aunt? _____

13. your mother's second husband's first wife's and his daughter? _____

14. your son's grandmother's brother's son's daughter? _____

15. your mother's nephew's son? _____

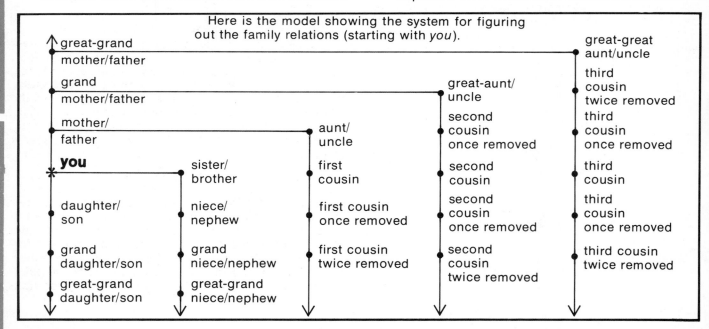

Here is the model showing the system for figuring out the family relations (starting with *you*).

| | | | | |
|---|---|---|---|---|
| great-grand mother/father | | | | great-great aunt/uncle |
| grand mother/father | | great-aunt/ uncle | | third cousin twice removed |
| mother/ father | aunt/ uncle | second cousin once removed | | third cousin once removed |
| **you** | sister/ brother | first cousin | second cousin | third cousin |
| daughter/ son | niece/ nephew | first cousin once removed | second cousin once removed | third cousin once removed |
| grand daughter/son | grand niece/nephew | first cousin twice removed | second cousin twice removed | third cousin twice removed |
| great-grand daughter/son | great-grand niece/nephew | | | |

**Also note:** A cousin *removed* is of a generation different from yours. The number the cousin is removed equals the number of generations away from yours.

Other definitions not shown: *stepmother/father*—parent married to a natural parent; *stepsister/brother*—child of the stepparent from a previous marriage; *half sister/brother*—child whose one parent is your natural parent and the other is your stepparent; *mother/father-in-law*—parent of your husband/wife; *brother/sister-in-law*—brother or sister of your husband/wife or wife/husband of your brother/sister.

## Exploratory Questions for Family Tree

Here is a family tree for a family we'll call Tree. It may be put on the board while students do Part I. Look at the numbered circles and find how they are related to the *you* in the tree.

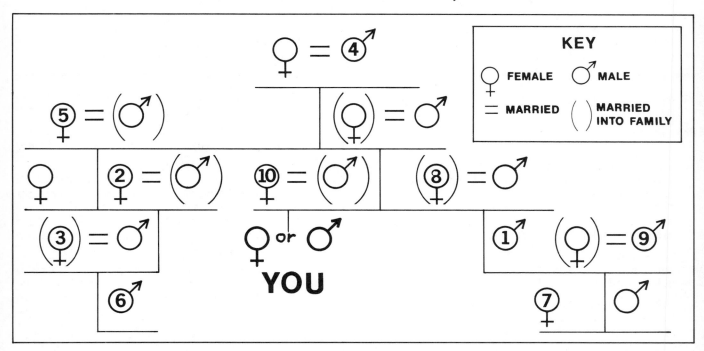

**Untangle these riddles:** A strange marriage: One day at a wedding, the father of a young woman became her husband's brother-in-law, and her husband's sister became her stepmother. How could this be?

How about this fishing trip? Two fathers and two sons went fishing. Each caught a beautiful fish, and none of them caught the same fish—but only three fish were caught. Explain.

### Answers to Questions on Student Page

1. your grandmother or no relation, if she is on the other side of the family
2. your great-grandmother or no relation
3. your stepmother
4. your first cousin
5. your nephew or son or no relation
6. your first cousin twice removed
7. your grandmother or great-aunt
8. yourself or no relation
9. your grandmother or no relation
10. your sister-in-law
11. your mother or aunt
12. your sister or yourself
13. your stepsister
14. your first cousin once removed or no relation
15. your first cousin once removed

### Answers to Tree Family

1. your first cousin
2. your second cousin once removed
3. your second cousin
4. your great-grandfather
5. your great-aunt
6. your second cousin once removed
7. your first cousin once removed
8. your aunt
9. your first cousin
10. your mother

### Answers to Riddles on Student Page

The wedding tale: The husband's sister married the wife's father.

The fish story: The men fishing were a grandfather, father, and son.

English

Social Studies

Class

Individuals

# GAME OF 26

*Here are pictures of twenty-six items —one for each letter of the alphabet. Think of these pictures as raw material to be molded into any activity you like. The following are some ideas of what can be done with these pictures.*

**Object:** Development of observation and memory skills

**Procedures:**

1. Have students study the pictures for one minute. Then have them write down as many items as they can remember (without looking at the pictures, of course). Present this activity as an experiment, and explain to the class that peeking at the pictures will interfere with the results. If you use an opaque projector, the problem of peeking will be solved!

2. Have the students repeat the above process, adding any pictures that they can remember after the second viewing.

3. Perhaps now go over all the pictures with the class to be sure that all students have the same word identification for each picture.

4. Again, have students, without looking at the pictures, write down items in the pictures that begin with any random letters, for example, *w, a, s, m, q.*

5. Have students repeat the first step described, and see if they can now remember all twenty-six items.

6. Have students take turns listing the items orally in alphabetical order. Each student has a turn and lists one. Do this individually or in teams.

**Object:** Development of observation of position and spatial relations

**Procedures:**

1. Have students put the pictures away, and ask them to describe the positions of the pictures. Which appeared in the lower left corner, the upper left corner, etc.? You may ask for answers out loud and write them on the board. Once all the positions are named, check back with the picture page. The comparison between what is remembered and what is real should be interesting! Are some students particularly good at remembering the positions of items?

2. Another way of practicing the observing of spatial relations is to ask students whether a particular drawing is at the top, the middle, the bottom, the left, and so forth of the page. For example, where is the rabbit? the giraffe? You should ask about five to ten items. Again, have the students write their own responses, or solicit answers and write them on the board.

3. Another question series in a similar vein involves asking which picture is on top of another one, next to another, or below another.

**Object:** Sharpening of categorizing and ordering skills

**Procedure:** Have the class categorize the twenty-six items in as many possible ways as they can. This activity can best be done in small groups. Have the class divide into teams of three to five members each. Have each team select a representative. Eventually, he will present the team's results to the entire class.

The team's task is to classify the pictured items in all conceivable ways. They can use any and all possible reference points. Categories may refer to the function of the item, its size, whether or not it is alive, its material composition, makeup of the word itself (number of letters, syllables), and the usefulness and popularity of the item. Let students use whatever reference materials are available in the classroom. The only criterion is that any category listed must contain at least two pictured items to qualify as a category.

Ten minutes or so before the period ends, have the representatives present their results. One point is given for each category mentioned, and one extra point for each category that no other team mentioned.

*Note:* If the class has difficulty getting started, give students some hints. Explain some of the possible categories, as given above.

**Object:** Sharpening of sentence and story writing skills.

**Procedure:** Students may use the pictures as the basis for writing sentences or stories. Have them write sentences using as many of these words as possible. Sentences, stories, or poems should be clever, funny, newsworthy, dramatic, or any other category the class and teacher may choose. After fifteen minutes or so, ask for volunteers to read their material. Have the class react to them, and perhaps select the ones that best fit each category.

Here is the alphabetical listing of the items in the pictures.

| | | | | |
|---|---|---|---|---|
| apple | giraffe | moon | star | Yo-Yo |
| balloon | hand | nest | tent | zebra |
| cards | iron | octopus | umbrella | |
| door | jacks | parachute | violin | |
| envelope | kite | quarter | watermelon | |
| fish | lamp | rabbit | xylophone | |

# GAME OF 26

English

Science

Social Studies

Class Groups

Individuals

Dittos*

# LETTER SLOTS

Make complete words, using the letters in the word *rain* together with the letters and spaces below. The letters of *rain* may be rearranged in any fashion, but the letters shown must be used as is. Example: Number 4 below is ce*rtain*.

1. st _ _ _ _ _

2. _ efr _ _ _

3. m _ _ g _ _

4. ce _ t _ _ _

5. g _ _ _ _ te

6. _ spi _ _ _

7. b _ _ _ _ _

8. _ sce _ ta _ _

9. _ _ t _ _ g

10. ba _ g _ _ _

Here's another set. Use the letters in *corn*.

1. a _ _ _ _ _

2. a _ c _ _ dio _

3. s _ _ _ pio _

4. _ _ _ w _

5. _ a _ t _ _

6. _ _ _ _ er

7. _ _ u _ t _ y

8. s _ _ _ _ _

9. _ _ u _ te _

10. _ a _ _ ati _ n

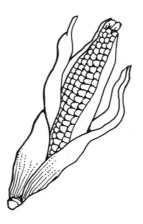

Now use the letters in *steam*. Five letters this time!

1. _ i _ _ _ k _

2. _ _ _ _ _ r

3. _ u _ _ _ ch _

4. p _ _ _ i _ _

5. _ _ r _ _ _

6. _ _ _ _ _ n

7. _ _ _ tr _ _ s

8. _ _ _ t _ _ ent

9. _ o _ _ rs _ ul _

10. _ h _ r _ o _ t _ t

Here, use the letters in *love*.

1. _ _ i _ _

2. s _ _ _ _ _

3. r _ _ _ _ _ t

4. n _ _ _ _ _

5. sh _ _ _ _ _

6. _ i _ _ _ nce

7. d _ _ e _ _ p

8. _ _ _ _ _ city

9. c _ _ _ _ r

10. _ _ e _ at _ r

Now, can you make up some of these sets?

## Answers to Letter Slots

**rain**
1. strain
2. refrain
3. margin
4. certain
5. granite
6. aspirin
7. brain
8. ascertain
9. rating
10. bargain

**steam**
1. mistake
2. master
3. mustache
4. pastime
5. stream
6. stamen
7. mattress
8. statement
9. somersault
10. thermostat

**corn**
1. acorn
2. accordion
3. scorpion
4. crown
5. carton
6. corner
7. country
8. scorn
9. counter
10. carnation

**love**
1. olive
2. solve
3. revolt
4. novel
5. shovel
6. violence
7. develop
8. velocity
9. clover
10. elevator

# MAGIC WORD SQUARES
## Solve Them! Make Them!

A magic word square reads the same across and down! In the first group below, fill in the empty cells with the letters given. Look at the hints. (Some words are plurals and proper nouns.)

Use d, n, n, n, n, s, s, t, v, v. Hint: One is where birds keep their young.

1.

| E |   | E |   |
|---|---|---|---|
|   | A |   | E |
| E |   |   |   |
|   | E |   |   |

Use a, a, a, e, e, d, m, m, n, n, r, r, s, s, t, t, w, w. Hint: One is a liquid. One is a place containing much of this liquid.

2.

| S |   |   | P |
|---|---|---|---|
|   |   | E |   |
|   | O |   |   |
|   | E |   |   |
| P |   |   | S |

Use e, e, m, m, o, o, t, t, t, t. Hint: One is an important road sign.

3.

| S |   |   | P |
|---|---|---|---|
|   | I |   |   |
|   |   | I |   |
| P |   |   | S |

Use h, m, m, r, r, s, s, v. Hint: One is where the heart is.

4.

|   | O |   | E |
|---|---|---|---|
| O |   | E |   |
|   | E |   | A |
| E |   | A |   |

Use d, f, h, i, i, l, l, l, n, n, n, r, r, r, r, s, s, u. Hint: One is a country. One is plural.

5.

|   |   | I |   | T |
|---|---|---|---|---|
|   |   |   | A |   |
| I |   |   |   | A |
|   | A |   |   |   |
| T |   | A |   |   |

Use a, a, a, d, d, e, e, g, g, h, o, o, r, r, s, s, t, t. Hint: One is plural. One is a means of communication.

6.

| G |   |   | P |
|---|---|---|---|
|   |   | I |   |
|   | A |   |   |
|   | I |   |   |
| P |   |   | S |

Now use the squares and words given to make magic word squares of your own. Use any letters you like.

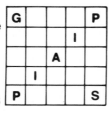

7.

| S | W | I | M |
|---|---|---|---|
| W |   |   |   |
| I |   |   |   |
| M |   |   |   |

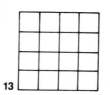

8.

| G | I | R | L |
|---|---|---|---|
| I |   |   |   |
| R |   |   |   |
| L |   |   |   |

9.

| N | I | C | E |
|---|---|---|---|
| I |   |   |   |
| C |   |   |   |
| E |   |   |   |

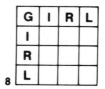

10.

| S | P | O | R | T |
|---|---|---|---|---|
| P |   |   |   |   |
| O |   |   |   |   |
| R |   |   |   |   |
| T |   |   |   |   |

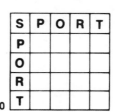

11.

| B | L | A | S | T |
|---|---|---|---|---|
| L |   |   |   |   |
| A |   |   |   |   |
| S |   |   |   |   |
| T |   |   |   |   |

12.

| F | E | A | S | T |
|---|---|---|---|---|
| E |   |   |   |   |
| A |   |   |   |   |
| S |   |   |   |   |
| T |   |   |   |   |

Finally, here's a chance for you to make your own magic word squares from scratch.

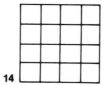
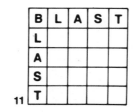
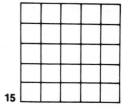

13.    14.    15.

Now, how about a 6x6 square. You're ready for it.

## Answers to Magic Word Squares

**1.** E V E N
V A N E
E N D S
N E S T

**2.** S W A M P
W A T E R
A T O N E
M E N D S
P R E S S

**3.** S T O P
T I M E
O M I T
P E T S

**4.** H O M E
O V E R
M E S A
E R A S

**5.** F L I R T
L U N A R
I N D I A
R A I N S
T R A S H

**6.** G R A S P
R A D I O
A D A G E
S I G H T
P O E T S

The following are sample answers, not the only possible answers.

**7.** S W I M
W I N E
I N K S
M E S S

**8.** G I R L
I D E A
R E S T
L A T E

**9.** N I C E
I D E A
C E N T
E A T S

**10.** S P O R T
P O L A R
O L I V E
R A V E N
T R E N D

**11.** B L A S T
L A T E R
A T O N E
S E N S E
T R E E S

**12.** F E A S T
E N S U E
A S P E N
S U E D E
T E N E T

# Memory Dial

**Object:** To teach an old and a well-known trick for improving memory of intrinsically meaningless but important material, like telephone numbers. The trick is to make the material itself meaningful, which will lead to easy memorizing. (See also *Sense Versus Non-sense,* page 106.) Phone numbers are a ready vehicle for doing this. Except for 1 and 0, the numerals of a telephone number have corresponding letters on the telephone dial. (See the drawing.) The trick is to make words out of these numbers. Such words, called *mnemonics,* are easier to remember than the numbers themselves.

**Materials:** Paper and pencil. Blackboard is helpful.

**Student groupings:** Individuals or small groups.

**Preparation:** Draw a telephone dial on the blackboard. Write some names of persons and their telephone numbers on the board. Examples for numbers that work well follow, but you may want to make up your own. Obviously some numbers are easier to work with than others, and some are probably impossible.

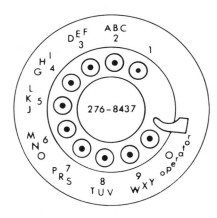

**Examples of numbers which work well:**

| Person | Number | Mnemonics |
|---|---|---|
| Mrs. Smith | 639-9675 | New York |
| Doctor | 945-3228 | wildcat |
| Jennifer | 276-8437 | brother |
| The movies | 373-4448 | freight |
| Pizza place | 447-2333 | his beef |
| Bob | 732-6887 | peanuts |
| Julie | 772-6474 | Spanish |
| Grandmother | 666-7837 | monster |
| School | 364-2483 | dogbite |
| Neighbor | 768-3700 | Rover-zero-zero |
| Library | 231-4373 | be-one-here |

**Procedure:** Students are to take the numbers given and try to convert them into words by substituting the corresponding letters for the numerals from the phone dial. One efficient method for doing this is to write the telephone number out and show the corresponding letters beneath it. For example,

```
6 3 9 - 9 6 7 5
M D W   W M P J
N E X   X N R K
O F Y   Y O S L
```

EQUALS *New York* or *new work!*

Because the numerals 1 and 0 have no corresponding letters and because *Q* and *Z* do not appear on the telephone dial, students may substitute *Q* for 1 and *Z* for 0—but they must remember that they did so! Otherwise, let the 1 and 0 remain and build the words around these obstacles.

After the class has worked on the given examples for a while (ten to fifteen minutes), have them compare their words in a discussion. Answers may be varied and of great interest.

Finally, and most important, have students try to make words out of their own telephone numbers and out of other numbers important to them.

Another trick that should be mentioned here, but need not be tackled if you have run out of time or it seems difficult or inappropriate, is to make the mnemonics particularly meaningful to the persons whose numbers they represent. For example, if Mrs. Smith's number is 639-9675 and the corresponding word is *New York* or *new work,* then the meaningful phrase might be "Mrs. Smith loves (hates) New York" or "Mrs. Smith is looking for new work." The more concrete the image, the better.

# MORSE CODE

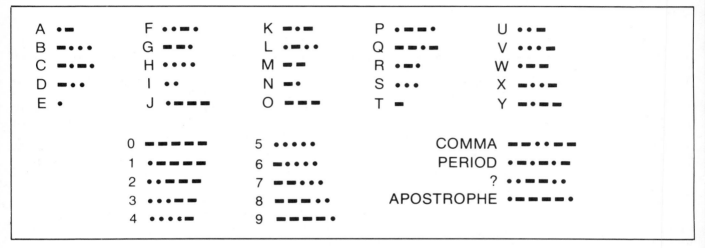

DahDah/ DahDahDah/ DiDahDit/ DiDiDit/ Dit/ /DahDiDahDit/ DahDahDah/ DahDiDit/ Dit//

Today you'll begin to learn how to use Morse code, the code of ham operators and telegraphers (and those of us who like to transmit secret messages).

Here are the alphabet, numbers, and a few other essential symbols:

| | | | | | | | | |
|---|---|---|---|---|---|---|---|
| A • ▬ | F • • ▬ • | K ▬ • ▬ | P • ▬ ▬ • | U • • ▬ |
| B ▬ • • • | G ▬ ▬ • | L • ▬ • • | Q ▬ ▬ • ▬ | V • • • ▬ |
| C ▬ • ▬ • | H • • • • | M ▬ ▬ | R • ▬ • | W • ▬ ▬ |
| D ▬ • • | I • • | N ▬ • | S • • • | X ▬ • • ▬ |
| E • | J • ▬ ▬ ▬ | O ▬ ▬ ▬ | T ▬ | Y ▬ • ▬ ▬ |

| | | | |
|---|---|---|---|
| 0 ▬ ▬ ▬ ▬ ▬ | 5 • • • • • | COMMA ▬ ▬ • • ▬ ▬ |
| 1 • ▬ ▬ ▬ ▬ | 6 ▬ • • • • | PERIOD • ▬ • ▬ • ▬ |
| 2 • • ▬ ▬ ▬ | 7 ▬ ▬ • • • | ? • • ▬ ▬ • • |
| 3 • • • ▬ ▬ | 8 ▬ ▬ ▬ • • | APOSTROPHE • ▬ ▬ ▬ ▬ • |
| 4 • • • • ▬ | 9 ▬ ▬ ▬ ▬ • | |

In the messages below, *one slant* appears between the letters of a word; *two slants* appear between words, before punctuation marks, and at the ends of sentences.

Now you're all set!

Answer these questions in Morse code:

Write your name in Morse code:

_____

Write your address in Morse code:

_____

_____

▬▬•/▬▬▬// ▬•▬•/▬▬▬/•▬•▬// •••/•▬/•••/•▬•//
▬▬▬•/▬••/▬▬▬•▬// •▬•/••▬/▬▬▬•▬//
•••/•▬••/•▬•//••/•▬•// •/▬▬//
▬▬•/•/▬▬▬// ▬▬▬/▬▬▬•/•/•// ▬▬•/•▬/▬▬/•/•••// •▬•▬•▬//

•▬▬/•••/•▬/▬▬// •/•/•••// ▬▬▬•/▬▬▬/•▬•//
•▬•/•••/•▬•/▬▬▬// •▬•/•/•••// ▬▬▬/▬▬▬/•▬•// •▬•▬•▬//

•▬▬/•••/•▬/▬▬// ▬▬•/•/▬▬▬// ▬▬▬•/▬▬▬•/•/▬▬// •▬•••/••/▬▬•/•//
▬•/•▬/▬▬•/•// ▬▬•/•/▬▬▬// •▬/▬▬•/•/•▬•// •/•▬•/•/•//
•••/▬▬▬•/•••/▬▬▬/▬▬▬/•▬••// ••▬•/•//

•▬▬/•••/•▬/▬▬// ••▬•/•▬•// •▬•/▬▬▬•// ▬▬▬•/▬▬▬/••▬//
•▬/•▬•/•/▬▬// ••▬•/••▬// ▬▬▬•/▬▬▬/▬▬•/••/•/•••//

▬▬•/•••/•▬/▬▬// ••/•••// ▬•/•▬/•▬// ▬▬•/•/•▬•/▬•/•••/•▬//
▬•/••/▬••/•// ▬▬▬•/▬▬▬/•▬•// ••▬•/•▬•▬•//

43

## The Morse Code Questions on the Student Page are

1. Do you have brothers or sisters? Give their names.
2. What is your favorite food?
3. What do you like to do after school?
4. Whom do you admire most?
5. What is the weather like today?

### Notes for the teacher

Because messages in Morse code are transmitted by sound, spend time in class relaying messages from one student to the rest of the class. Morse code may be transmitted by any clicking sound, such as a pencil tap on a desk. For dits (dots), pause a short while between clicks; for dahs (dashes), leave a longer space; and between words, leave still longer intervals of time.

### Questions for discussion

Ask students whether they can detect any system in the code symbols. Which are the simplest symbols? the most complex? Put the following table on the blackboard.

Table of English letters in order of their frequency in words:

| E | → D | → W |
|---|---|---|
| T | L | B |
| A | F | V |
| O | C | K |
| N | M | X |
| R | U | J |
| I | G | Q |
| S | Y | Z |
| H | P | |

During the discussion, you should arrive at the understanding that this code is based *more or less* on the English language: The simplest letters appear most frequently; the most complex, least often. Ask why Morse code is based on English and discuss its history, including its origin in the United States. If there are any hams in the class, you may want to talk about amateur radio operating.

# Say what you mean, mean what you say...

Here's an activity that is challenging, enjoyable, and has an immediate payoff: students show significant improvement in communication skills during a single class period!

**Object:** To give students practice in the precise use of language. Students have to describe verbally to their classmates something that is visual, and, conversely, draw something that is described verbally. Through this practice, they learn precision in giving and taking instructions.

**Materials:** Bring to class several nonrepresentational designs. Some ready-to-use examples appear on the following pages. All students should have paper and pencil (or a pen) at their desks.

**Procedure:** One student is selected. (Let students volunteer, or pick someone randomly.) You show the student one design. (Any other designs on the same piece of paper should be shielded from him.) The student is given a few moments to study the design. He may not show it to any of the other students. As soon as he has studied the picture, he begins his task of verbally explaining it to his classmates so that they, by merely listening, will be able to duplicate it on their papers. As he talks, they draw. He may refer to the picture as often as he wishes. He may use only words —no gestures. Students may question him as he goes along. After a given amount of time (no more than five minutes), all students end their efforts. The student who explained the design shows it to the class; his classmates then compare their efforts with the model. Size, details, and shapes all matter!

After the students have seen one anothers' designs, another student is chosen to be the design reporter and the entire process is repeated. After several of the examples brought in by you have been used, you may wish to let each student make a design. Have the class repeat the exercise with self-made designs.

By the end of the period, students will usually show significant improvement both in how they give directions and in how they take them. Hopefully, directions such as "Draw a big circle" or "Put the triangle next to the dot." will have been replaced with more precise ones. Students will say what they mean and mean what they say!

FOLD BACK

FOLD BACK

M-M-M-M-M-M

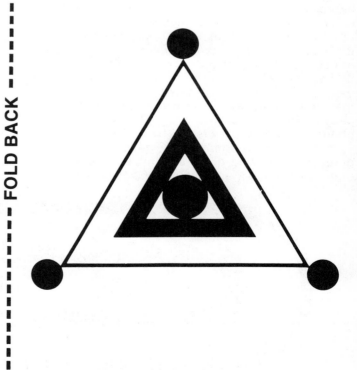

English

Math Language Foreign

Class

Other

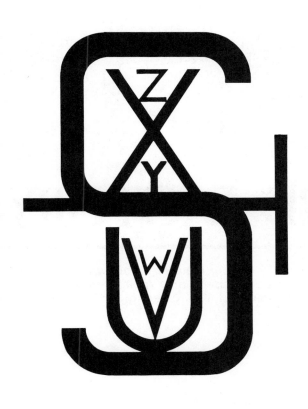

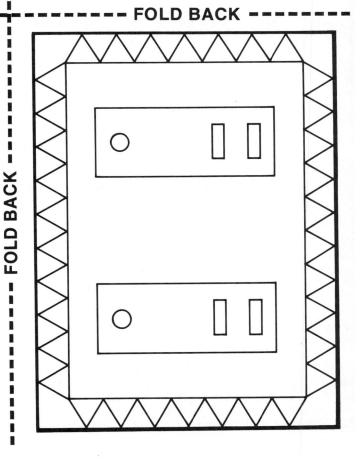

Foreign
English Language Math

Class

Other

# YE OLDE WORD FACTORY

You are about to go into the business of manufacturing words! All the raw materials are here: prefixes, roots, and suffixes. You are to combine one of each—a prefix from List 1, a root from List 2, and a suffix from List 3—for every word that you make. Please use a dictionary as your manual. If your words are to pass inspection (in spect ion), spelling must be correct. The meanings of all parts are given for your information.

| List 1 | List 2 | List 3 |
|---|---|---|
| a, an (not, without) | dic, dict (say) | able (worthy of) |
| bi (twice, two) | duc, duct (lead) | ible (being, being able) |
| con, com (with, together) | graph (write) | ary (pertaining to, connected with) |
| de (off, away) | ject (throw) | ate (act, condition of being) |
| ex (off, out of) | log (talk, knowledge) | ation (state, condition) |
| im, in (into, in toward) | plic, ply (fold) | ator (one who) |
| intra (within) | port (carry) | er (one who) |
| oc, ob, op (against) | sect (cut) | ion (state, condition) |
| re, red (back, again) | spec, spect (look, see) | ive (having the quality of) |
| pre (before) | tact, tang (touch) | ment (result, means) |
| tele (far, distant) | trac, tract (draw) | or (one who) |
| trans (across) | vert, vers, verse (turn) | y (characterized, is inclined to) |
| un, im, in (not) | | |

Here are a few examples: pre  dict  able (able to say before)

re port er (one who carries back)

Now see what you can do. How many words can you manufacture?

When it is time to display your product, that is, your list of words, explain how each word obtains its meaning from its three parts. Do this either in teams or individually. The person or team who has the longest list of words and can explain their meanings is the winner.

## Some Example Words for Ye Olde Word Factory

1. bi sect ion—state of being cut in two.
2. con duct or—one who leads with.
3. de port ation—state of being carried away.
4. ex tract ion—state of drawing (pulling) out.
5. in ject ion—state of throwing into.
6. ob ject ion—state of throwing against (now, being against).
7. pre dict ion—state of saying before.
8. tele graph y—inclined to write far.
9. in tang ible—being unable to touch.
10. re vers ible—being able to turn back.

These are only examples. There are many more possibilities.

# THE BODY

## EL CUERPO – LE CORPS

These scrambled words are parts of the body. Unscramble their spellings to form words in the language you are studying; then, see if you can match each with its English translation (listed in alphabetical order on the right side of the page.) Finally, try it in the other language—you'll find many similarities! The Spanish and French articles for masculine or feminine are given.

| Spanish | French | English |
|---------|--------|---------|
| **1.** (la) oamn _____ | (la) anim _____ | _____ arm |
| **2.** (los) balois _____ | (les) vèrsel _____ | _____ back |
| **3.** (el) ozócran _____ | (le) ourec _____ | _____ chest |
| **4.** (la) diralol _____ | (le) ugeno _____ | _____ chin |
| **5.** (la) lipe _____ | (la) epua _____ | _____ ear |
| **6.** (el) ipe _____ | (le) iped _____ | _____ elbow |
| **7.** (la) zabace _____ | (la) êett _____ | _____ eye |
| **8.** (el) ooj _____ | (le) elio _____ | _____ eyebrow |
| **9.** (el) poel _____ | (les) hveecux _____ | _____ finger |
| **10.** (la) craitun _____ | (la) creitune _____ | _____ foot |
| **11.** (la) naperi _____ | (la) mebaj _____ | _____ hair |
| **12.** (el) tendie _____ | (la) tend _____ | _____ hand |
| **13.** (la) abbarlli _____ | (le) notmen _____ | _____ head |
| **14.** (la) jaec _____ | (le) ricouls _____ | _____ heart |
| **15.** (la) sdeapal _____ | (le) sdo _____ | _____ knee |
| **16.** (la) cabo _____ | (la) cobheu _____ | _____ leg |
| **17.** (la) jareo _____ | (la) loleeri _____ | _____ lips |
| **18.** (el) oded _____ | (le) digot _____ | _____ mouth |
| **19.** (la) nagelu _____ | (la) nagelu _____ | _____ neck |
| **20.** (el) horbmo _____ | (la) leapué _____ | _____ nose |
| **21.** (el) hocep _____ | (la) rotineip _____ | _____ shoulder |
| **22.** (el) locuel _____ | (le) ocu _____ | _____ skin |
| **23.** (el) zorba _____ | (le) sarb _____ | _____ tongue |
| **24.** (la) zairn _____ | (le) zen _____ | _____ tooth |
| **25.** (el) dooc _____ | (le) doecu _____ | _____ waist |

Foreign Language

Class

Individuals

Dittos*

50

## Answers to the Body—El Cuerpo—Le Corps

| | | |
|---|---|---|
| **1.** | (la) mano—la main (hand) | 23 arm |
| **2.** | (los) labios—les lèvres (lips) | 15 back |
| **3.** | (el) corazón—le coeur (heart) | 21 chest |
| **4.** | (la) rodilla—le genou (knee) | 13 chin |
| **5.** | (la) piel—la peau (skin) | 17 ear |
| **6.** | (el) pie—le pied (foot) | 25 elbow |
| **7.** | (la) cabeza—la tête (head) | 8 eye |
| **8.** | (el) ojo—l'oeil (eye) | 14 eyebrow |
| **9.** | (el) pelo—les cheveux (hair) | 18 finger |
| **10.** | (la) cintura—la ceinture (waist) | 6 foot |
| **11.** | (la) pierna—la jambe (leg) | 9 hair |
| **12.** | (el) diente—la dent (tooth) | 1 hand |
| **13.** | (la) barbilla—le menton (chin) | 7 head |
| **14.** | (la) ceja—le sourcil (eyebrow) | 3 heart |
| **15.** | (la) espalda—le dos (back) | 4 knee |
| **16.** | (la) boca—la bouche (mouth) | 11 leg |
| **17.** | (la) oreja—l'oreille (ear) | 2 lips |
| **18.** | (el) dedo—le doigt (finger) | 16 mouth |
| **19.** | (la) lengua—la langue (tongue) | 22 neck |
| **20.** | (el) hombro—l'épaule (shoulder) | 24 nose |
| **21.** | (el) pecho—la poitrine (chest) | 20 shoulder |
| **22.** | (el) cuello—le cou (neck) | 5 skin |
| **23.** | (el) brazo—le bras (arm) | 19 tongue |
| **24.** | (la) nariz—le nez (nose) | 12 tooth |
| **25.** | (el) codo—le coude (elbow) | 10 waist |

## For Further Enrichment

With a well-behaved class, you could follow this activity with *Simon Says!* in Spanish *(Simon Dice!)* or French *(Simon Dit!)*. The students will enjoy the chance to get up and stretch, but you must be able to enjoy the added noise and activity—otherwise, skip this suggestion!

You could also explore with the class the patterns of similarities among the three languages: English, Spanish, and French. Follow the procedure we describe in *The Living Room—Le Salon—La Sala (page 53 and 54).*

# THE LIVING ROOM
## Le Salon-La Sala

Experiment in both French and Spanish! How many words do you know in *both* languages? You'll be surprised! How similar are they?

A living room is pictured below. At the sides of the room are the words for the numbered items in the living room; the words are scattered on the page, and first parts of the words are separated from last parts. Words are not necessarily divided by syllables.

You are to find the words by connecting first and last parts and listing them so each word matches the number it represents. Two examples in each language are given. The parts of the words are used once. Cross each off after you have used it.

Work first in the language you are studying. Then try the other language!

French

FEN LAM CH RES POR TÉLÉ EN CHAI AT FLEU SO FA RS SE PEIN LIV TURE PE CAR ÉTRE MU PETTE VISION MU LOGE TR TAB HOR R CHI LE

Spanish

RED GA PIN SIL FÁ TO PUER SA RO TELE PARA ES ROS RE ALFORM BRA SO TANA TURA ME PA LÁM PER TA VISIÓ LOJ FLOR LA VT LIB VEN

Le Salon (French Living room) _____

1. (la) porte _____
2. (la) horloge _____
3. (la) _____
4. (le) _____
5. (la) _____
6. (la) _____
7. (la) _____
8. (les) _____
9. (les) _____
10. (le) _____
11. (la) _____
12. (la) _____
13. (le) _____
14. (le) _____
15. (la) _____

La Sala (Spanish living room)

1. (la) puerta _____
2. (el) reloj _____
3. (la) _____
4. (la) _____
5. (la) _____
6. (la) _____
7. (la) _____
8. (las) _____
9. (los) _____
10. (el) _____
11. (la) _____
12. (la) _____
13. (el) _____
14. (el) _____
15. (la) _____

## Answers to The Living Room—Le Salon—La Sala

| English | French | Spanish | English | French | Spanish |
|---------|--------|---------|---------|--------|---------|
| 1. the door | la porte | la puerta | 9. the books | les livres | los libros |
| 2. the clock | la horloge | el reloj | 10. the sofa | le sofa | el sofá |
| 3. the painting | la peinture | la pintura | 11. the lamp | la lampe | la lámpara |
| 4. the wall | le mur | la pared | 12. the television | la télévision | la televisión |
| 5. the window | la fenêtre | la ventana | 13. the dog | le chien | el perro |
| 6. the chair | la chaise | la silla | 14. the cat | le chat | el gato |
| 7. the table | la table | la mesa | 15. the carpet, rug | la carpette | la alfombra |
| 8. the flowers | les fleurs | las flores | | | |

### For discussion

Have students work in pairs or in small groups. Help them. Give them hints—even answers—if they seem to be struggling. (This would be an especially good idea in the second language!) This first half of the puzzle (putting the words together) should take about half the period. You may, of course, choose to do only this part. Then, the entire period may be spent on it.

Next, use the words the class and you have listed to make comparisons between English, French, and Spanish. Which words are the same or similar in French and Spanish?

| French | Spanish |
|--------|---------|
| la porte | la puerta |
| les fleurs | las flores |
| les livres | los libros |
| le sofa | el sofá |
| la horloge | el reloj |
| la lampe | la lámpara |
| la télévision | la televisión |
| le salon | la sala |

**There are eight of these.**

Which words are the same or similar in French and English?

| French | English |
|--------|---------|
| la peinture | the painting |
| la chaise | the chair |
| la table | the table |
| les fleurs | the flowers |
| le sofa | the sofa |
| la lampe | the lamp |
| la télévision | the television |
| le chat | the cat |
| la carpette | the carpet |

**There are nine of these.**

Which words are the same or similar in Spanish and English?

| Spanish | English |
|---------|---------|
| la pintura | the painting |
| las flores | the flowers |
| el sofá | the sofa |

la lámpara        the lamp

la televisión      the television

**There are five of these.**

Ask the students if they can draw any conclusion from these similarities. For example, ask which language, French or Spanish, is more like English. When students say that French seems to be, ask whether such a conclusion is valid. Remind the class that they have seen similarities between only a few words and have not dealt with enough words to make a valid generalized statement.

In some cases, both the French and Spanish words are similar to their English cognates

le salon, la sala, the salon

les livres, los libros, library

la porte, la puerta, the portal

You may want to ask students to compare English words with those of still other languages. Here are the words already used translated into Italian (a Romance language) and German.

| English (the living room) | Italian (il soggiorno) | German (das Wohnzimmer) |
|---|---|---|
| 1. the door _____ | la porta _____ | die Tür |
| 2. the clock _____ | l' orologio _____ | die Wanduhr |
| 3. the painting _____ | la pittura _____ | das Bild |
| 4. the wall _____ | la parete _____ | die Wand |
| 5. the window _____ | la finestra _____ | das Fenster |
| 6. the chair _____ | la sedia _____ | der Stuhl |
| 7. the table _____ | la tavola _____ | der Tisch |
| 8. the flowers _____ | i fiori _____ | die Blumen |
| 9. the books _____ | i libri _____ | die Bücher |
| 10. the sofa _____ | il sofà _____ | das Sofa |
| 11. the lamp _____ | la lampada _____ | die Lampe |
| 12. the television _____ | la televisione _____ | das Fernsehen |
| 13. the dog _____ | il cane _____ | der Hund |
| 14. the cat _____ | il gatto _____ | die Katze |
| 15. the rug, carpet _____ | il tappeto _____ | der Teppich |

What observations and comparisons can you and the class now make? Explore!

# Add-A-Letter
## Ajoutez-Une-Lettre

Add a letter to the word at the left to get an example of or a synonym for the word at the right. Letters may be left in the same order or rearranged.

**Now try making up some of these puzzles!**

Example: Add a letter to (l')âme—soul to get comrade—amie.

1. (le) mot-word _____ n'avoir pas de vie _____
2. rendre-to return _____ antonyme de donner _____
3. (l')orage-thunderstorm _____ un fruit _____
4. (le) chemin-road _____ un appareil combiné pour produire certains effets _____
5. (le) repas-meal _____ traverser _____
6. mai-May _____ ☞ _____
7. aimer-to like, love _____ un propriétaire, directeur _____
8. (la) main-hand _____ une partie du jour _____
9. (le) chat-cat _____ une mélodie _____
10. coûter-to cost _____ prêter l'oreille pour entendre _____
11. (la) vache-cow _____ une autre animal _____
12. (le) fièvre-fever _____ un mois d'année _____
13. lire-to read _____ 📖 _____
14. le-the _____ une petite pièce de terre _____
15. (la) lèvre-lip _____ porter de bas en haut _____
16. aider-to aid, help _____ vite _____
17. ouvrir-to open _____ un homme qui travail _____
18. (la) table-table _____ une danse _____
19. (le) soir-evening _____ un numéro _____
20. (le) mari-husband _____ un jour de la semaine _____
21. (le) divan-divan, couch _____ quelque chose à manger _____
22. (le) coeur-heart _____ par exemple, blanc, noir, rouge (add 2 letters) _____
23. beau-beautiful _____ ⬡ (Add 2 letters) _____
24. vrai-true _____ un ennemi _____
25. une-one _____ ce qui donne la lumière pendant la nuit _____

Foreign Language

Individuals

## Answers to *Add-A-Letter–Ajoutez une Lettre*

1.  (la) mort
2.  prendre
3.   (l') orange
4.  (la) machine
5.  passer
6.  (la) main
7.  (le) maître
8.  (le) matin
9.  (le) chant
10. écouter
11. (le) cheval
12. (le) février
13. (le) livre
14. (l') île
15. élever
16. rapide
17. (l') ouvrier
18. (le) ballet
19. trois
20. (le) mardi
21. (la) viande
22. (la) couleur
23. (le) bateau
24. (le) rival
25. (la) lune

# FRENCH CULTURE

Here are four puzzles dealing with various aspects of French culture. In each one, think of names that belong in the given category, and fit them vertically in the letter boxes. The first three words are filled in as an example. The puzzle makes no sense horizontally. Use books, encyclopedias, maps, and so on.

Cities of France

Which is the capital? Which is the home town of a famous mustard? Which name is in the French national anthem?

Authors and Poets

Painters

About 80,000,000 people in the world speak French. In which countries are they a majority of the population? Ten countries are in Africa. One is in the Americas. Four are in Europe. Why are so many in Africa?

## Answers to French Culture

The rows of ***** indicate spaces on the puzzle.

*Villes de France (Cities of France)*
Versailles
Calais
Lyons
Le Havre
Caen
Orleans
********
Dijon
Bordeaux
********
Clermont-Ferrand
Cherbourg
Paris
Amiens
Cannes
Marseille

Paris is the capital of France. Dijon is the home of the mustard. Marseille is in the French national anthem, "La Marseillaise."

*French-Speaking Countries*
France
Cameroon
Belgium
Guinea
Chad
Haiti
*******
Congo
Luxembourg
Upper Volta
Gabon
Switzerland
Mauritania
Mali
Dahomey
Senegal

In the Americas: Haiti. In Europe: France, Belgium, Luxembourg, Switzerland. All the others are in Africa. They are former French colonies.

*Auteurs et Poètes (Authors and Poets)*
Zola
Hugo
Flaubert
Montaigne
Camus
Rimbaud
Rabelais
********
Gide
La Fontaine
***********
De Maupassant
Villon
Molière
Proust
Corneille
Sartre

*Les Peintres (Painters)*
Rouault
Degas
Pissaro
*******
Poussin
Cezanne
Chardin
Monet or Manet
Watteau
Renoir
Courbet
Matisse

# FRENCH LETTER SLOTS

Use the letters of the French word (la) *main* to make words of the following items. The letters can be used in any order, but each may be used only once per word and all must fit the given blanks.

1. (la) _ _ _ s o _
2. (l') _ _ _ _ _ a l
3. (le) c _ _ é _ _
4. d e _ _ _ _ _
5. (la) s e _ _ _ _ _ e
6. (le) _ _ t _ _
7. (le) d _ _ _ _ _ c h e
8. _ _ _ g i _ e r
9. (la) _ o _ n _ _ e
10. _ _ _ _ n t e _ a n t
11. (le) _ _ g a s _ _
12. _ _ p o r t _ _ t
13. (la) _ _ c h _ _ e

Here are some words with the letters of *rire*.
Fill in the letters properly.

1. c _ o _ _ _
2. _´ c _ _ _ e
3. (le) m _ _ c _ e d _
4. (le) t _ _ _ a _ n
5. (le) q u a _ t _ _ _
6. (le) p _ e m _ _ _
7. (le) d e _ n _ _ _ _
8. a _ r _ v _ _
9. (la) p _ _ _ _ e
10. (la) p _ a _ _ i _

Now do the same with the letters of (le) *chat.*

1. _ _ _ e _ e r
2. (le) _ _ _ n _
3. (le) y _ _ _ _ _
4. (le) _ _ o c o l _ _
5. _ _ t a _ _ e r
6. _ _ _ n _ e r
7. (le) _ _ r i _ o _
8. m é _ _ _ n _
9. _ _ _ r m a n _
10. (le) _ _ _ _ l e _

Now use the letters of (le) *coeur.*
*Note:* There are five letters this time.

1. (la) _ _ _ l _ u _
2. (la) f _ _ _ _ h _ t t e
3. (la) s _ _ _ _ _ _
4. _ _ ^ t _ _
5. _ _ _ _ c h _ _
6. _´ _ _ _ t e _
7. (le) m _ _ _ _ a _
8. _ _ c _ p _ _
9. (le) b _ _ _ h _ _

59

## Answers to French Letter Slots

| La Main | | The Hand | Le Chat | | The Cat |
|---|---|---|---|---|---|
| **1.** | (la) maison | house | **1.** acheter | to buy |
| **2.** | (l') animal | animal | **2.** (le) chant | song |
| **3.** | (le) cinéma | cinema | **3.** (le) yacht | yacht |
| **4.** | demain | tomorrow | **4.** (le) chocolat | chocolate |
| **5.** | (la) semaine | week | **5.** attacher | to attach |
| **6.** | (le) matin | morning | **6.** chanter | to sing |
| **7.** | (le) dimanche | Sunday | **7.** (le) haricot | kidney bean |
| **8.** | imaginer | to imagine | **8.** méchant | wicked |
| **9.** | (la) monnaie | money | **9.** charmant | charming |
| **10.** | maintenant | now | **10.** (le) chalet | chalet |
| **11.** | (le) magasin | store | | |
| **12.** | important | important | | |
| **13.** | (la) machine | machine | | |

| Rire | | To Laugh | Le Coeur | | The Heart |
|---|---|---|---|---|---|
| **1.** | croire | to believe | **1.** (la) couleur | color |
| **2.** | écrire | to write | **2.** (la) fourchette | fork |
| **3.** | (le) mercredi | Wednesday | **3.** (la) source | source |
| **4.** | (le) terrain | ground | **4.** coûter | to cost |
| **5.** | (le) quartier | quarter | **5.** coucher | to put to bed |
| **6.** | (le) premier | first | **6.** écouter | to listen |
| **7.** | (le) dernier | last | **7.** (le) morceau | piece |
| **8.** | arriver | to arrive | **8.** occuper | to occupy |
| **9.** | (la) pierre | stone | **9.** (le) boucher | butcher |
| **10.** | (la) prairie | meadow | | |

# LES ALIMENTS ↔ LES ALIMENTS

## THE FOODS   THE FOODS

Below are the names of twenty foods in French, but they are hard to read! Each letter (except *i*) is missing one line. Fill in the proper lines, and you'll read these foods easily. Lines are horizontal, vertical, or diagonal.

Note that each letter is not always shown in the same way.

After you have discovered the words, fit them into the proper categories below.

1. *(la)* ΓΓPΠ⁻ I Ξ
2. *(le)* I ΠI I
3. *(le)* PΓI I FI
4. *(la)* ΒHI IΠΛΞ
5. *(le)* PΓIΞϽΠI I
6. *(les)* PϝIΞII IϚ
7. *(le)* PIΞ
8. *(la)* ϽI HΓΞ
9. *(le)* EÊ I FFL
10. *(le)* ΓϽΠVHϹF
11. *(la)* PUΜΜΞϽΞ ⁻ΞRRF
12. *(le)* PΠIΛ
13. *(le)* ΒUFLΓ
14. *(la)* PUΜIVΞ
15. *(la)* ⁻UΜΠI F
16. *(l')* ϹRΠI IϝΞ
17. *(la)* /IFI ϽF
18. *(le)* PΠPΓ
19. *(les)* IIFRIΠϹϚ /ΞPIϚ
20. *(le)* ΒFLRRΞ

**Fruit**
1. _____
2. _____
3. _____
4. _____

**Starch**
1. _____
2. _____
3. _____

**Vegetable**
1. _____
2. _____
3. _____
4. _____

**Meat and Fish**
1. _____
2. _____
3. _____
4. _____
5. _____

**Dairy**
1. _____
2. _____
3. _____
4. _____

**Answers to Les Aliments**

1. (la) carotte (carrot)
2. (le) lait (milk)
3. (le) poulet (chicken)
4. (la) banane (banana)
5. (le) poisson (fish)
6. (les) raisins (grapes)
7. (le) riz (rice)
8. (la) glace (ice cream)
9. (le) gâteau (cake)
10. (le) fromage (cheese)
11. (la) pomme de terre (potato)
12. (le) pain (bread)
13. (le) boeuf (beef)
14. (la) pomme (apple)
15. (la) tomate (tomato)
16. (l') orange (orange)
17. (la) viande (meat)
18. (le) porc (pork)
19. (les) haricots verts (green beans)
20. (le) beurre (butter)

| Fruit | Starch | Vegetables | Meat and Fish | Dairy |
|---|---|---|---|---|
| 1. (la) pomme | 1. (le) pain | 1. (la) pomme de terre | 1. (le) porc | 1. (la) glace |
| 2. (la) banane | 2. (le) riz | 2. (la) carotte | 2. (le) poulet | 2. (le) fromage |
| 3. (les) raisins | 3. (le) gâteau | 3. (la) tomate | 3. (le) beouf | 3. (le) lait |
| 4. (l') orange | | 4. (les) haricots verts | 4. (la) viande | 4. (le) beurre |
| | | | 5. (le) poisson | |

# Add-A-Letter
## Agregue-Una-Letra

Add a letter to the word at the left to get an example of a synonym for the word at the right. Letters may be left in the same order or rearranged.

Example: Add a letter to (la) cosa to get coast—costa.

1. (la) mañana-morning _____
2. (la) madre-mother _____ (a product made from trees) _____
3. (el) año-year _____
4. (el) tren-train _____ (a direction) _____
5. (el) medio-middle _____ (a doctor) _____
6. (la) radio-radio _____ (fast, quick) _____
7. creer-to believe _____ (to grow) _____
8. (el) taco-taco _____ (someone in a movie) _____
9. real-royal _____ (a part of the alphabet) _____
10. (el) banco-bank _____ (a color) _____
11. tiene-has _____ (a number) _____
12. tocar-to play an instrument; to touch _____ (a number) _____
13. ella-she _____ (used to open a door) _____
14. loco-crazy _____ (for example, red, blue, green) _____
15. estar-to be _____ (to sit down) _____
16. tres-three _____ (verb of being) _____
17. tarde-late _____ (behind) _____
18. (el) estado-state _____ (a place in which sports are played) _____
19. frío-cold _____ (fried) _____
20. (la) casa-house _____ (to take out) _____
21. (el) polo-pole _____ (poultry) _____
22. entre-between _____ (entire, whole) _____
23. caro-expensive _____
24. (la) nube-cloud _____ (good) _____
25. (el) oro-gold _____ (a color) _____

Now, see how many of these you can make up.

## Answers to *Add-A-Letter–Agregue-Una-Letra*

1. (la) manzana
2. (la) madera
3. (la) mano
4. (el) norte
5. (el) médico
6. rápido
7. crecer
8. (el) actor
9. (la) letra
10. blanco
11. veinte
12. cuarto
13. (la) llave
14. (el) color
15. sentar
16. estar
17. detrás
18. (el) estadio
19. frito
20. sacar
21. (el) pollo
22. entero
23. (el) barco
24. bueno
25. rojo

# LAS COMIDAS ↔ ΙΠ5 ΓCΜIΠ75

## THE FOODS    ⊤⊢Ξ ⅎCϽϽ5

Below are the names of twenty foods in Spanish, but they are hard to read! Each letter (except *i*) is missing one line. Fill in the proper lines, and you'll read these foods easily. Lines are horizontal, vertical, or diagonal.

Note that each letter is not always shown in the same way.
After you have the words, fit them into the proper categories below.

---

1. (*la*) ⌐ΓΓⱻ
2. (*el*) ΡΠΙΙ
3. (*el*) ΡⵊⵊⵊϽϹ
4. (*el*) ΡΙΝΙΞΙΙΠ
5. (*el*) ΙΙⱻΙΠϽϹ
6. (*el*) ΓΓΙϽΠΙ
7. (*la*) ΜΠΙΙ7ⅎΝⅎ
8. (*la*) ΓⅎΡΝΞ
9. (*la*) ΜⅎΝⵊΞϽLΙΙΙⅎ
10. (*el*) ΝⅎΡΙϽΓϹ

11. (*la*) 7ⅎΙΙⅎΙΙϹΡΙⅎ
12. (*la*) ΡΠΙⅎ⌐Η
13. (*el*) ϹLΞⱻϹ
14. (*el*) ΡϽΙΙϹ
15. (*la*) Lⵊⅎ
16. (*el*) ⅎΓΡϹⱻ
17. (*la*) ΙΙⅎΡΠΙΙϽΠ
18. (*el*) ⌐ϹΜΠΙΞ
19. (*el*) ϽΙΓΙⅎⅎ
20. (*el*) ΡⅎΙΙϹϹLΞΠΙΙⅎ

**Fruit**
1. _____
2. _____
3. _____

**Starch**
1. _____
2. _____
3. _____

**Vegetables**
1. _____
2. _____
3. _____
4. _____
5. _____

**Meat and Fish**
1. _____
2. _____
3. _____
4. _____
5. _____

**Dairy**
1. _____
2. _____
3. _____
4. _____

### Answers to *Las Comidas*

1. (la) leche (milk)
2. (el) pan (bread)
3. (el) pescado (fish)
4. (el) pimiento (pepper)
5. (el) helado (ice cream)
6. (el) frijol (bean)
7. (la) manzana (apple)
8. (la) carne (meat)
9. (la) mantequilla (butter)
10. (el) marisco (shellfish)
11. (la) zanahoria (carrot)
12. (la) patata (potato)
13. (el) queso (cheese)
14. (el) pollo (chicken)
15. (la) uva (grape)
16. (el) arroz (rice)
17. (la) naranja (orange)
18. (el) tomate (tomato)
19. (el) biftec (beef)
20. (el) panqueque (pancake)

Fruit
1. (la) manzana
2. (la) uva
3. (la) naranja

Starch
1. (el) pan
2. (el) arroz
3. (el) panqueque

Vegetables
1. (el) pimiento
2. (el) frijol
3. (la) zanahoria
4. (la) patata
5. (el) tomate

Meat and Fish
1. (el) pescado
2. (la) carne
3. (el) marisco
4. (el) pollo
5. (el) biftec

Dairy
1. (la) leche
2. (el) helado
3. (la) mantequilla
4. (el) queso

# SPANISH CULTURE

Here are five puzzles that deal with various parts of Spanish culture. Each one requires that you think of words that belong to a given category and fit these items *vertically* in the letter boxes. Three words are filled in as an example.

Almost 200,000,000 people in the world speak Spanish. In which countries are they in the majority? Which continent are most of these countries in? Why is this?

La Semana

Days of the Week

Which day is missing?

Spanish Painters, Writers, and Musicians

Capitals of Spanish-Speaking Countries . . . . . .

throughout the world

Las Comidas

Popular Foods of Spain and Mexico

## Answers to *Spanish Culture*

The rows of ******* indicate spaces in the puzzle.

Spanish-Speaking Countries
Spain
Peru
Paraguay
Venezuela
Nicaragua
El Salvador
Chile
***********
Cuba
Colombia
Uruguay
Panama
Argentina
Costa Rica
Bolivia
Mexico
Honduras

All the countries here are in Central and South America (except Spain). Latin America was colonized by Spaniards.

Les Capitales
Capitals of Spanish-Speaking Countries Throughout
the World

| | |
|---|---|
| Lima | Peru |
| Buenos Aires | Argentina |
| Sucre | Bolivia |
| ************* | |
| Caracas | Venezuela |
| Santiago | Chile |
| Panama | Panama |
| Madrid | Spain |
| Quito | Ecuador |
| Havana | Cuba |
| Tegucigalpa | Honduras |
| Montevideo | Uruguay |
| San Juan | Puerto Rico |

Days of the Week
lunes
jueves
miércoles
sábado
domingo
martes
Missing is viernes.

Spanish Painters, Writers, and Musicians
Lorca
Miro
Cervantes
Casals
*********
El Greco
*********
Segovia
Picasso
Velazquez
Dali
Jimenez

Las Comidas     Popular Foods
paella
taco
tostada
********
chorizo
guacamole
maíz
tortilla
enchilada
gazpacho
frijoles

68

# SPANISH LETTER SLOTS

Use the letters of the Spanish word (la) *mano* to make words of the following items. The letters can be used in any order, but each may be used only once per word and all must fit the given blanks.

1. (el) _ l u _ _ _
2. (la) _ _ _ t a ñ _
3. (el) h e r _ _ _ _ _
4. (la) _ _ _ _ e d
5. (el) _ e x i c _ _ _ _
6. (el) _ _ _ _ d a t _
7. s _ l _ _ e _ t e
8. (la) c e r e _ _ _ _ i
9. (el) a _ e r i c _ _ _
10. (el) c _ _ a r _
11. (el) c _ _ i _ _ 
12. (el) c _ _ i _ _

Complete these words using the letters of the word *tres.*

1. c o n _ _ _ _ t a _
2. _ _ _ a _
3. d _ _ _ á _
4. (el) m a _ _ _ _ _
5. n e c _ _ i _ a _
6. (el) p o _ _ _ _
7. n u _ _ _ _ o
8. (la) _ _ _ _ e l l a
9. (la) _ u e _ _ _
10. _ _ i _ t _
11. (el) m a _ _ _ _ o
12. (el) i n _ _ _ e _

Now do the same with the letters of (el) *taco.*

1. (el) _ e n _ _ v _
2. _ u _ n _ _ ?
3. _ _ s _ _ r
4. (el) _ r _ f i _ _
5. (la) _ _ r b _ _ a
6. _ _ n _ _ r
7. (la) n _ _ i _ i
8. _ _ h e n _ _
9. _ _ e n _ i _ n
10. (la) e s _ _ _ i _ n
11. (el) _ u _ r _ _
12. _ _ _ _ _ r
13. e x _ _ _ _ _

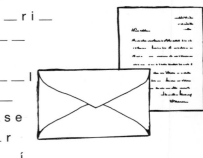

Now use the letters of (la) *carta.*
Note: There are five letters this time!

1. _ _ e p _ _ _ _
2. (la) s e _ _ e _ _ r i _
3. (la) _ o _ b _ _ _ _
4. _ _ n _ _ _ _
5. (la) _ _ _ e d _ _ l
6. _ u _ _ e n _ _
7. _ _ o s _ _ _ _ s e
8. _ _ p _ u _ _ r
9. (la) _ _ f e _ e _ í _

---

Now see how many of these sets of letter slots you can make up.

**69**

## Answers to *Spanish Letter Slots*

### La Mano — The Hand

1. (el) alumno — student
2. (la) montaña — mountain
3. (el) hermano — brother
4. (la) moneda — coin
5. (el) mexicano — Mexican
6. (el) mandato — command
7. solamente — only
8. (la) ceremonia — ceremony
9. (el) americano — American
10. (el) camarón — shrimp
11. (el) camión — truck
12. (el) camino — road

### Tres — Three

1. contestar — to answer
2. estar — to be
3. detrás — behind
4. (el) martes — Tuesday
5. necesitar — to need
6. (el) postre — desert
7. nuestro — our
8. (la) estrella — star
9. (la) suerte — luck
10. triste — sad
11. (el) maestro — teacher
12. (el) interés — interest

### El Taco — The Taco

1. (el) centavo — cent
2. cuánto? — how much?
3. costar — to cost
4. (el) tráfico — traffic
5. (la) corbata — necktie
6. contar — to count
7. (la) noticia — news
8. ochenta — eighty
9. atención — attention
10. (la) estación — station
11. (el) cuarto — room
12. tocar — to touch, play an instrument
13. exacto — exact

### La Carta — The Letter

1. aceptar — to accept
2. (la) secretaria — secretary
3. (la) corbata — necktie
4. cantar — to sing
5. (la) catedral — cathedral
6. cuarenta — forty
7. acostarse — to go to bed
8. capturar — to capture
9. (la) cafetería — cafeteria

# Dicey Tic Tac Toe

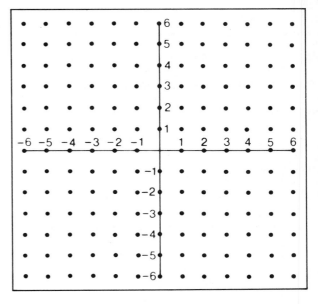

**Object:** To place four marks in a row.

**Materials:** One or more pair of dice.

**Student groupings:** With one pair of dice, divide the class into two teams. With more than one pair, divide the class into two teams per pair of dice.

**Preparation:** On the blackboard, draw an array of points as shown. If several games are proceeding simultaneously each pair of teams may make their own arrays on the board or on paper at their seats.

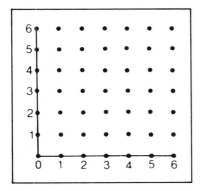

**The play:** Teams take turns shooting a pair of dice. One member of the team who's turn it is shoots the dice. He may then choose which number pair he wishes to use. That is, if one die shows 5 and the other 4, he may mark point (5, 4) *or* point (4, 5). However, he must call out one or the other number pair, and he must mark the one he has called out. Thus, if he calls out (5, 4) and marks (4, 5) which is $x = 4$, $y = 5$, he loses his turn. One team indicates its points by circling them. The other team indicates its points by putting an X on them. Members of competing teams alternate turns. Scoring: The first team to place four marks in a straight line— (horizontal, vertical, or diagonal)—wins.

**Variations:** This game may be played in four quadrants in various ways. The array of points is as shown. Each player may choose positive or negative signs for the two dice. That is, he may call (+5, −4), (−5, −4), (+4, −5), or so forth. This variation expands the play and increases its interest for experienced students.

If the class has had a great deal of experience plotting number pairs, the game may be made more interesting by using two pair of dice, each pair a different color. (If you use spinners rather than dice, you will need two spinners. *See* next paragraph.) Before you begin, have the class decide that one color will represent the first number of the pair, and the second color will represent the second number. Students will now have up to four possible number pairs to choose from. For example, if there are two red dice and two white dice, a student may decide that the red die will be the horizontal (or first number), and the white die the vertical (or second number of the number pair). For example, if someone throws four dice and obtains a red 6, a red 4, a white 2, and a white 3, the possible number pairs are (6, 2), (6, 3), (4, 2) and (4, 3). The student may choose any of these four pairs as his move. However, when students play this way, they must retain the order of the pairs; they cannot, for example, use (6, 2) *or* (2, 6). Once the horizontal color has been established, it cannot be changed. And, as before, after a student names the number pair he has chosen, he must locate that point correctly or lose his turn.

71

**Variations in which dice are not used:** If dice are not available, you may make an adequate spinner from an index card and a paper fastener. Cut off an edge, ⅜ inch wide, from one end of the index card, and shape it into an arrow. Punch a hole as close to its center of gravity as you can. (Determine this point by balancing the arrow on your finger. The point at which it balances will be fairly close.) Put the paper fastener through this hole and through the card, and fasten it loosely. The arrow should spin fairly well. The finished spinner should look like the example shown. Two spins determine the two numbers to be plotted.

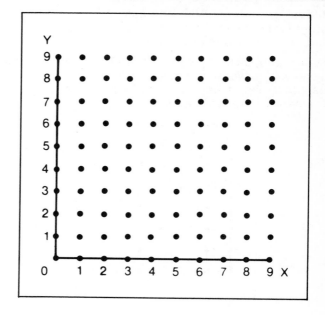

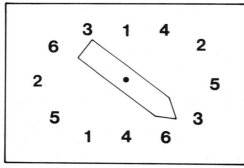

You can generate numerals for number pairs without using dice or a spinner. To do this, you will need a fair sized book and a coin. Have students flip to any page in the book. Then have them flip the coin; if the coin shows heads, the student looks at the right hand page, if it shows tails, he looks at the left-hand page. The number he uses is the last digit of the page number. Discuss with the students why they should flip the coin as well as the pages. Ask them what about the last digit of every right-hand page. (It will always be odd.) Use of the coin and the page flip satisfactorily randomizes the numbers. Whereas the dice only generate numerals 1 to 6, this method will generate numerals 0 to 9. This means the game is played on a larger array of points. For example, the first quadrant game board will look like this:

# FIBONACCI

This is a fascinating number sequence that was first described by an early thirteenth century Italian mathematician, Leonardo Fibonacci. It occurs unexpectedly and frequently in nature and in mathematics. For example, the florets of a daisy head form two opposite sets of rotating spirals. There are 21 spirals clockwise and 34 counterclockwise. This 21:34 ratio corresponds to two adjacent terms in the mysterious Fibonacci sequence. Pine cones form a 5:8 spiral formation, and the spirals of a pineapple are 8:13:21.

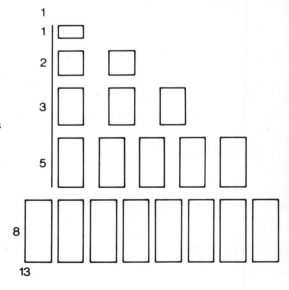

# SEQUENCE

### The Fibonacci Bricklayer

You are building a path with bricks that are 1 by 2 units in size. Your path is 2 units wide at every stage.

Fill in the *different* ways you can arrange your bricks to fill the space at each stage; when the path is one unit long, then 2 units long, then 3 units long, then 4, 5, 6, . . . units long.

Notice the number of different possible arrangements at each stage generates the Fibonacci sequence.

Fill in the blanks in the following Fibonacci sequence:
1, 1, 2, 3, 5, __, 13, 21, __, __, __, __, __, __, __, __, . . . .
Trace the Fibonacci sequence through the following mazes:

If you X out the squares of the Fibonacci sequence, you will find one letter of the inventor's name revealed. Which is it?

| 3 | 5 | 8 | 13 |
|---|---|---|---|
| 2 | 7 | 6 | 21 |
| 1 | 18 | 9 | 34 |
| 1 | 89 | 55 | 65 |
| 144 | 113 | 408 | 4181 |
| 233 | 303 | 579 | 2584 |
| 377 | 610 | 987 | 1597 |

If you X out the squares of this sequence which starts 1, 4, . . . and proceeds as a Fibonacci sequence (that is, to obtain the next term, you add the two preceding numbers), you will obtain a number in the Fibonacci sequence that you worked with in the other maze. Which number is it?

| 9 | 5 | 4 | 1 |
|---|---|---|---|
| 14 | 13 | 21 | 58 |
| 23 | 37 | 60 | 65 |
| 35 | 40 | 87 | 97 |
| 75 | 87 | 175 | 157 |
| 1076 | 756 | 250 | 254 |
| 1056 | 665 | 411 | 387 |

Size of space to be filled in units of length.

Your bricks are 1 by 2 units in size. This is a picture of one of them.

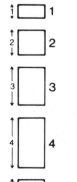

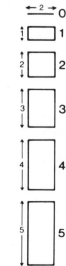

Can you continue the path for 6 and beyond?

How many different ways can you fill it?

Picture the ways. (Brick in the un-bricked paths.)

Notice the symmetries involved in the arrangements.

## Answers to Fibonacci Sequences on the Student Page:

Each term in the Fibonacci sequence is equal to the sum of the preceding two terms. Therefore, the first fifteen terms of the sequence are 1, 1, 2, 3, 5, *8*, 13, 21, *34, 55, 89, 144, 233, 377, 610,* . . .

The solutions to the mazes are *B* and 5.

The bricklayer's problem may be used as a class activity. Here are the solutions:

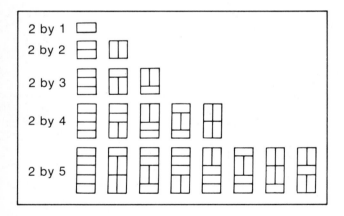

## Exploratory Activities

This is an easy activity to do without the ditto. Here are some ways you might proceed.

1. Put the Fibonnaci mazes on the board before class.

2. Have a student put the mazes on the board as you are talking about the sequence and explaining the rule for generating it. You will need some ingenuity to sketch on the board or describe the daisy head that appears on the ditto. It is worth the effort to do this, for this is an example of how the Fibonacci sequence appears in nature. If you can bring a pine cone into the class to pass around, that would be an excellent example—provided you can read the swirls. It's a little tricky! The skin of a pineapple will also show a part of the sequence.

3. At the least, tell how the sequence is generated, and have the students continue to generate it. While they are doing this, draw the Fibonnaci mazes on the board. As students are doing these puzzles, you could be planning how you will introduce the Fibonacci bricklayer.

4. Here is a number trick based on the Fibonacci Sequence. Try it on the class, and see whether anyone can figure out how it works. Ask the class to list the numbers 1 through 10 on their papers. This is to help them keep track of the steps of the sequence they will be generating. Call on a member of the class to write two fairly small whole numbers on the blackboard. Everyone in the class, but you, can see them. (You keep your back to the board.) The class records these numbers, as the first two of their list of ten numbers. The numbers are erased from the board, and the student sits down and records them also. Ask the class to fill in the remaining eight places of their list, using the Fibonacci method of addition; that is, the third number is the sum of the first two, the fourth number is the sum of two and three, and so on.

When the class has reached their seventh entry, ask two people what their seventh number is, saying something like "It's very easy to make a silly mistake in addition. Number tricks are often spoiled by such mistakes, so let's make sure we're all OK up to here." When the class has reached the tenth number, ask students to add all ten numbers. Then you flash the sum out of thin air. (Write it on a slip of paper, beforehand). The class should be properly impressed. Do it again with different numbers. Again you will seem to have special information because you can give the correct answer although it is not always the same as in some number tricks. The answer will differ according to the original two numbers chosen. The trick is simple. The sum of the first ten numbers is equal to eleven times the seventh number from the class.

Using algebra, you can see how this works: Let *a* be any number. Let *b* be any other number. (Keeping *a* and *b* small merely facilitates the addition.) These are the ten numbers expressed in terms of *a* and *b:* 1st number = *a*, 2nd number = *b*, 3rd number = *a* + *b*, 4th number = *a* + 2*b*, 5th number = 2*a* + 3*b*, 6th number = 3*a* + 5*b*, 7th number = 5*a* + 8*b*, 8th number = 8*a* + 13*b*, 9th number = 13*a* + 21*b*, 10th number = 21*a* + 34*b*.

Add numbers 1 through ten, which equals 55*a* + 88*b*. Notice that number 7 is 5*a* + 8*b*. Notice also that 11 times 5*a* + 8*b* = 55*a* + 88*b*, = sum of first ten numbers.

Using values for *a* and *b*, let *a* = 3 and *b* = 4. Then we have 1st number = 3, 2nd number = 4, 3rd number = 7, 4th number = 11, 5th number = 18, 6th number = 29, 7th number = 47, 8th number = 76, 9th number = 123, 10th number = 199. The sum of these numbers is 517 = 11 × 47, where 47 is the seventh number.

**References:** Martin Gardner, "Mathematical Games, the Multiple Fascinations of the Fibonacci Sequence," *Scientific American, 220,* 116, March, 1969; Harold R. Jacobs, *Mathematics, A Human Endeavor,* W. H. Freeman, San Francisco, 1970; *Fibonacci Quarterly Journal,* The Fibonacci Association, San Jose State University, San Jose, California.

# flow diagrams

Social Studies Science Math

Individuals Groups Class

Blackboard

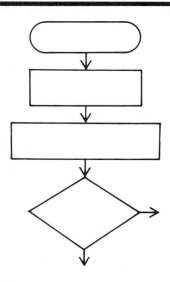

1. Leave home     4. Walk
2. Look at the clock     5. Catch a bus
3. Is it late?     6. Arrive at school

## The flow diagram looks like this:

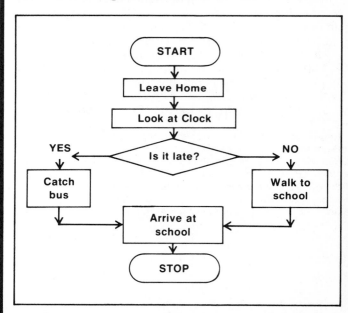

**What Are They?** A flow diagram may be thought of as a road map. A road map helps you find your way through unfamiliar terrain; a flow diagram helps you find your way through a computer program. In computer programming, a flow diagram may be a first stage in showing all the steps necessary to solve a problem.

If you want to use a road map, you must learn how to read it. This is true also for a flow diagram. Different computer languages use different symbols to represent different types of activities. For a start, let's agree on certain symbols:

means *start* or *stop*.

signifies an *operation;* that is, *do* something.

means make a *decision*. Notice that this is phrased as a question that requires a decision.

These symbols are connected by directed straight lines. Here is an example of a simple flow diagram showing how a student gets to school. The student leaves home for school each day. On the way out, he looks at the clock. If it is early, he walks to school. If it is fairly late, he catches a bus.

Notice that statement 3 which asks "Is it late?" is different from the other statements. (It is enclosed in a diamond shape.) This is a decision statement. It leads to two paths, a *yes* path and a *no* path. Such decisions are phrased as questions that can be answered by a simple yes or no. This restriction arises from the nature of computers, which operate by switching on or switching off electrical circuits. There are only these two possible states.

A question that requires more than two choices must be broken down for the program. A good example of such a procedure is the puzzle problem at the end of this section.

## Activities

**1.** Explore the flow diagrams already shown. Show the shapes for Start or Stop, ⬭, etc. Perhaps put the procedure for getting to school on the blackboard. Near it, draw the flow diagram shapes, but do not fill in the steps.

Ask the students to copy the diagram, and fill in the steps. Or have them take turns coming to the blackboard to fill in the steps.

Here is a flow diagram for crossing the road.

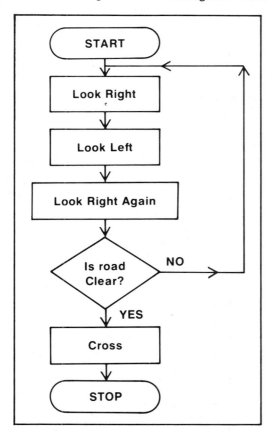

Follow the same process with the crossing-the-road procedure.

**2.** Have the class suggest some other situations suitable for flow diagramming. One example is the procedure for watching television: (1) Turn on the television; (2) Is it too loud—yes (turn knob; ask again)—no (go on); (4) Is the program OK—yes (go on); no (change channel; ask again); (5) Watch television.

Other procedures suitable for flow diagramming are buying and eating an ice cream cone, running and taking a bath, frying an egg, and making a long-distance telephone call.

**3.** Get class agreement on the succession and clarity of the statements. What decision statements are likely to arise? Make a list of these. Is your diagram such that anyone new to the procedure can follow the succession without ambiguity? Don't forget, a computer is a very stupid animal. It only knows how to do exactly what it is told to do. And it is only equipped to make decisions that have been carefully mapped out.

**4.** Divide the class into small groups. After discussing the general ideas with the class, you might divide the class into small groups to work on developing their own flow diagrams on the subjects they choose. Allow time toward the latter half of the period for the class to share and criticize one another's diagrams.

### Using Flow Diagrams in Mathematical Problems

Triangles may be classified as:

equilateral—The measure of all three sides is the same.

isosceles —The measure of two of the three sides the same.

scalene —The measure of all three sides is different.

Have students write a flow diagram to generate this classification. First make certain that the students understand the three classes of triangles:

equilateral   

isosceles   

scalene

Do students understand the decisions that have to be made? They should arrive at something like this:

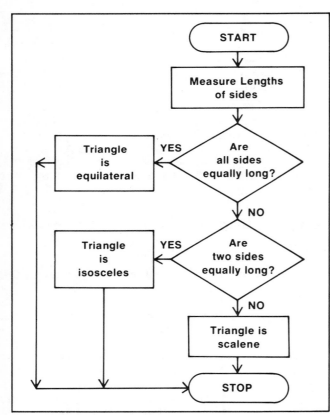

The diagram shown gives the procedure for measuring the perimeter of a triangle.

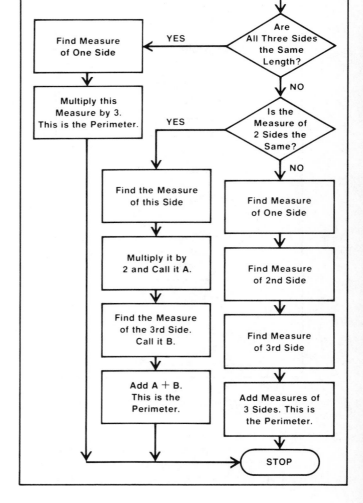

A flow diagram can be used to determine the perimeter of a geometric figure. Remember that the perimeter of a figure is the linear measure around the boundary of the figure. For a triangle, the measure is the sum of the lengths of the three sides. For example, the perimeter of this triangle

is $2 + 3 + 4 = 9$.

## A Puzzle

Here's a problem that lends itself beautifully to flow diagramming. Let the class try it.

One student thinks of a number from 1 to 20. By asking no more than five questions (answers only yes or no) discover the number.

Can the class make a flow diagram showing the procedure? Here is the diagram:

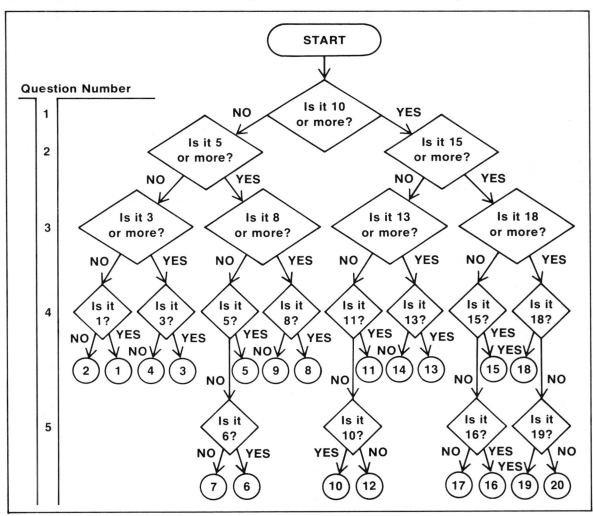

# Forest Fire Fighters

In the forest of the frizzy firs, fires form straight lines. Can students discover the relationship of the coordinates of the points of a straight line?

**Object:** To put out the forest fires of the opposition team in the shortest possible number of turns.

**Materials:** Graph paper and pencil (or pen). (Copy suitable for reproducing graph paper is supplied on page 99.)

**Student groupings:** Two teams. This may be done in various ways. The class may be divided into two teams, Team A and Team B. Team A has the fire in its forest. Team B tries to put it out. Or the class may be divided into smaller groups, several groups competing simultaneously.

**The Play:** Members of Team A mark 4 points each along two or three straight lines. Each of these points represents a burning frizzy fir. (If the class is divided into small teams (two against two,) you may use only one or two fires at each turn to speed up the game). The members of Team B take turns calling number pairs. If the number pair called locates a fir, the first team calls "On". If the number pair does not locate a fir, the call is "Miss." When the fire along one line is out, the first team calls "Fire out." When all the fires are out, the turn of Team B is over. The roles are now reversed; it is now Team B's turn to locate the burning trees, and Team A is the fire fighting team, calling number pairs.

**Scoring:** A recorder keeps track of the number of number pairs called before the fires are completely out. After both teams have completed their turn, the team with the *lowest* score wins. A team that calls the same number pair more than once is charged double for that call. Thus, it is a good idea for the team members trying to locate the burning trees to mark their papers at each number pair they call (perhaps X for "Miss" and 0 for "On") at the point indicated by the number pair. This will help them avoid calling the same pair more than once, and also keep track of the play.

**Examples:**

1. Team A places its burning trees as shown in the diagram. (This is a four-quadrant game.) The burning trees of fire *a* are at (0, −1), (1, 0), (2, 1), (3, 2).

The burning trees of fire B are at (1, 1), (0, 1), (−1, 1), (−2, 1). The burning trees of fire C are at (−2, 0), (0, 1), (2, 2), (4, 3).

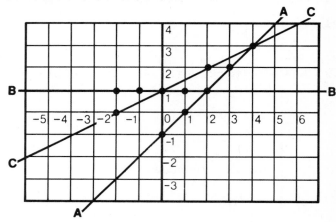

2. This is an easier game—a first quadrant game—with both numbers in the number pair positive. Team A places its burning trees as shown in the figure. The burning trees of fire A are at (2, 0), (4, 1), (6, 2), (8, 3). The burning trees of fire B are at (2, 3½), 4, 3), (6, 2½), (8, 2).

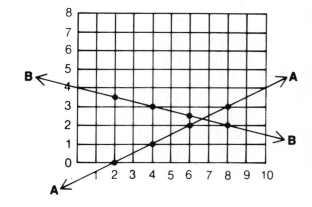

# FOUR-COLOR PROBLEM

Here's a chance for you to work on a famous problem in mathematics that hasn't been solved yet. The conjecture (or guess) is that it is possible to use only four different colors to color *any* map so that no two adjacent (neighboring) areas are the same color. We know it is important to color maps so that adjacent countries can be distinguished from one another.

It has been proved that five colors are sufficient to color any map. But no one has yet proved or disproved the theorem that maps of *any* number of regions can be colored with only four colors. (It has already been proved that four colors are sufficient for maps containing less than thirty-eight regions.) By the way, all you need do to disprove this theorem (and become world famous in the process) is find *one single* case in which the theorem fails. That is, if you could produce a map that cannot be colored with four different colors such that no two adjacent borders have the same color, you will have sucessfully disproved the theorem. One counterexample (and that is what you would have produced) would be enough to lay the theorem to rest. So go to it!

You may use the map of Africa, which is included in this book, as your map. However, you don't really need anything this complex to work on the problem. A general statement of the problem would permit you to arbitrarily divide any sheet of paper into regions by drawing random boundaries. When you have a satisfactory looking "map," begin work.

If you don't have five colors handy, either use a code, as shown, or use numerals 1, 2, 3, 4, 5 to represent the colors.

Here is an example:

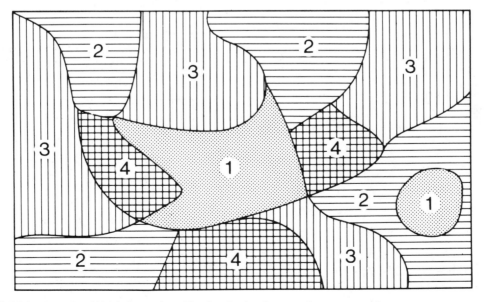

## Activities

**1.** Color the map of Africa. (See page 132)

**2.** Work in pairs. Each student may draw a random map as described above. Then the two students may exchange maps and try to disprove the theorem.

# KARD KAPERS

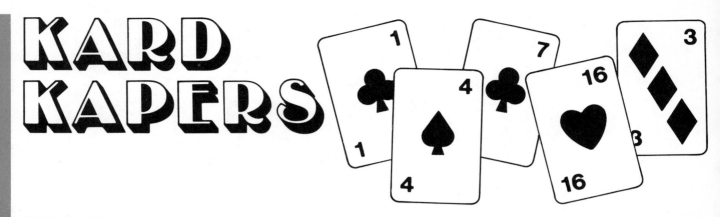

**Object:** To determine how many of the mathematical sentences below can be completed, using *all* the numbers on the cards above, combined with the elementary operations of arithmetic. (addition, subtraction, multiplication, and division).

**Example:**

$$\square\ \square\ \square\ \square\ \square = 1$$
$$\square\ \square\ \square\ \square\ \square = 2$$
$$\square\ \square\ \square\ \square\ \square = 3$$
$$\square\ \square\ \square\ \square\ \square = 4$$
$$\square\ \square\ \square\ \square\ \square = 5$$
$$\square\ \square\ \square\ \square\ \square = 6$$
$$\square\ \square\ \square\ \square\ \square = 7$$
$$\square\ \square\ \square\ \square\ \square = 8$$

Possible Solutions are:

$$(3 + 1) + (16 \div 4) - 7 = 1$$
$$[(7 \times 4) + 3 + 1] \div 16 = 2$$
$$[(1 + 16) - 7] - 4 - 3 = 3$$
$$(16 \times 3) \div (7 + 4 + 1) = 4$$
$$7 - [(16 \div 4) - 3] - 1 = 5$$
$$[(16 - 4) \times 3] \div (7 - 1) = 6$$
$$(16 + 3) - (7 + 4 + 1) = 7$$
$$(16 - 4 + 3 - 7) \div 1 = 8$$

**Student groupings:** Divide the class into groups of four, five, or more. Students may work together to develop solutions.

**Scoring:** The first solution using all five cards earns five points for the team. If the class has trouble getting started, give smaller number of points for solutions using fewer than all five cards. For example,

$$\square\ \square\ \square\ \square\ \square = 5$$

is the problem. Have the class form this sentence using 2, 4, 6, 8, 10. Score five points for a solution using all five numbers. For example,

$$\boxed{10} - \{\boxed{4} + [(\boxed{8} - \boxed{6} \div \boxed{2})]\} = 10 - \{4 + [2 \div 2]\} = 10 - 5 = 5$$

Score three points for a solution using four numbers. If the numbers are 2, 4, 8, 10, for example,

$$[(\boxed{10} - \boxed{2}) \div \boxed{8}] + \boxed{4} = [8 \div 8] + 4 = 1 + 4 = 5$$

Score two points for a solution using 3 numbers—for example using 4, 8, 10:

$$[(\boxed{4} \times \boxed{10}) \div \boxed{8}] = 40 \div 8 = 5$$

Remember, there are many other possible solutions for these problems. The ones presented here are merely examples.

**Variations:**

**1.** Try playing Kard Kapers using other combinations of five numbers! How many mathematical sentences can students make using 3, 3, 6, 5, 2?

$$[(6 - 5) + (3 \div 3)] - 2 = [1 + 1] - 2 = 0$$
$$[(6 - 5) + (3 \div 3)] \div 2 = [1 + 1] \div 2 = 1$$
$$(3 - 3) + 2(6 - 5) = 0 + 2 = 2$$
$$(3 \div 3) + 2(6 - 5) = 1 + 2 = 3$$
$$(3 \div 3) + (6 - 5) + 2 = 1 + 1 + 2 = 4$$
$$3 + (6 - 5) + (3 - 2) = 3 + 1 + 1 = 5$$
$$[(3 - 2) + (6 - 5)] \times 3 = [1 + 1] \times 3 = 6$$
$$[(3 + 3) - 6] + 5 + 2 = 0 + 5 + 2 = 7$$
$$[(3 + 3) \div 6] + 5 + 2 = [6 \div 6] + 5 + 2 = 8$$
$$3 + 6 + [5 - (2 + 3)] = 9 + 0 = 9$$
$$3 + 6 + [5 \div (2 + 3)] = 9 + [5 \div 5] = 10$$

To convince you that solutions are by no means unique, we have worked out several different solutions to

☐ ☐ ☐ ☐ ☐ = 1 using 3, 3, 6, 5, 2.

$(3 \times 6) - [(3 \times 5) + 2)] = 18 - [15 + 2] = 1$

$3 - [(6 - 5) + (3 - 2)] = 3 - [1 + 1] = 1$

$(6 \times 2) \div [(5 \times 3) - 3] = 12 \div [15 - 3] = 1$

$[(3 \div 3) + (6 - 5)] \div 2 = [1 + 1] \div 2 = 1$

$[6 \div 3] - [(2 + 3) \div 5] = 2 - 1 = 1$

$[5 - 3] - [6 - (2 + 3)] = 2 - 1 = 1$

2. This variation is for experts: Kard Kapers can be played using large numbers! For example, here are two solutions combining 7, 8, 16, 25, and 4 to make 5:

$$25 \div [16 - (8 + 7) + 4] = 5$$

$$[25 - (16 + 4)] \times (8 - 7) = 5$$

3. Have students use the first five counting numbers (1, 2, 3, 4, 5) to see how many numbers starting from zero they can make, using the basic operations. (We've reached into the 20's, and no end is in sight.)

4. Kard Kapers may be played using other arithmetic operations. For example, using exponentiation, $(1)^3 + 16 - 4 - 7 = 6$.

5. Take the digits of the year we're in. How many number sentences can students make using four digits, such as 1, 9, 7, and 3? Possible, but not unique, solutions are

$[(7 + 3) - 9] - 1 = 1 - 1 = 0$

$[(7 + 3) - 9] \div 1 = 1 \div 1 = 1$

$[(7 + 3) - 9] + 1 = 1 + 1 = 2$

$3 \div [(9 - 7) - 1] = 3 \div [2 - 1] = 3 \div 1 = 3$

$(9 - 7) + (3 - 1) = 2 + 2 = 4$

$(9 - 7) + (3 \div 1) = 2 + 3 = 5$

83

# LINES to CURVES

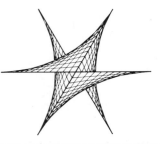 

Using a straight edge, *connect* the numbers that are the same. Make your own design in the empty square!

There is no limit to the number of designs you can create. You'll need more paper here.

Math

Class

Individuals

Dittos*

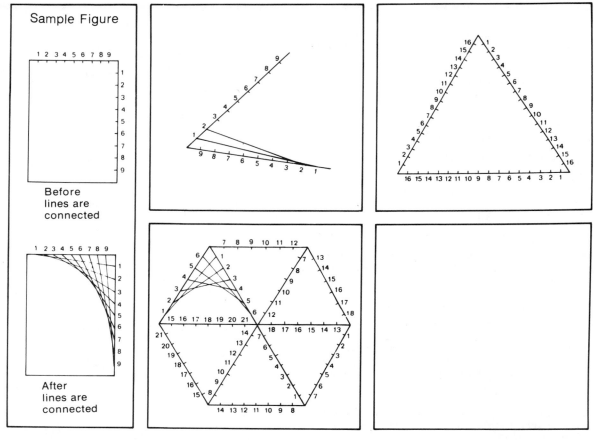

Sample Figure

Before lines are connected

After lines are connected

**DISCOVER!**
What happens when you increase or decrease the size of your angle?

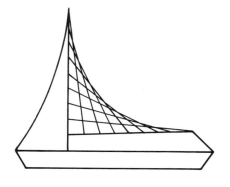

What happens when you increase or decrease the number of divisions along your line?

Analyze the designs at the top of the page together or alone. Can you see how they were done? Can you duplicate them?

Experiment with different shapes; make designs, and color them! Try using your initials for a starter.

**Reference for the teacher:** For an inexpensive collection of these designs, which can act as an excellent source of inspiration, see Dale G. Seymour and Joyce Snider, *Line Designs*, Creative Publications, Palo Alto, Calif. 94302).

# MATH QUICKIES

## RUSSIAN PEASANT MULTIPLICATION

Here's a neat example of a multiplication algorithm that is very different from the usual one students learn in school. Show the class how it works. See whether the students can make it work for them.

**Problem:** To multiply 15 by 13.

**Procedure:** Have students write two columns of numbers. The first column will be headed by one of the multipliers. Each entry will be half of the one above it. (Drop any fractions that may result from halving an odd number; that is, 13 becomes 6 when it is halved, and 7 becomes 3). The second column will be headed by the second multiplier. Each entry here will be double the one preceding it. Students should continue doubling until the adjacent number in the left-hand column is 1. Now, have them <u>cross out in the doubles column any number adjacent to an even number in the halves column.</u> This rule also applies to the row containing the original numbers. Have students add the remaining numbers in the doubled column. That sum will be the product of the original two numbers.

Students may check their answers by ordinary multiplication:

| 15 times | 13 |
|---|---|
| 7 | 26 |
| 3 | 52 |
| 1 | 104 |
| | 195 |

None crossed out because there are no even numbers in first column.

Check:

| 15 |
|---|
| 13 |
| 45 |
| 15 |
| 195 |

Notice what would have happened had the columns been reversed:

| 13 times | 15 |
|---|---|
| ~~6~~ | ~~30~~ |
| 3 | 60 |
| 1 | 120 |
| | 195 |

The answer is the same.

Here is another example:

| ~~230~~ times | ~~17~~ |
|---|---|
| 115 | 34 |
| 57 | 68 |
| ~~28~~ | ~~136~~ |
| ~~14~~ | ~~272~~ |
| 7 | 544 |
| 3 | 1088 |
| 1 | 2176 |
| Check: | 3910 |

Even numbers are crossed out.

Check:

| 230 |
|---|
| 17 |
| 1610 |
| 230 |
| 3910 |

Ask students to suggest problems, but not with excessively large numbers. These can certainly be done, but they may be clumsy.

## JORDAN CURVE THEOREM

Here's an interesting puzzle in topology. Draw something like this on the board:

Ask students to draw such a curve.

This is called a plane closed curve. It is a curvy, wavy or ridgy line that moves around in space and connects back to where it started. Be careful, however. This must be a *simple* closed curve. At no place may the boundary cross over itself. (No crossed lines!)

If students have difficulty understanding, have them consider a closed circle made of string. Then have

them bend the string any way they like. The only restriction is that it may not cross itself anywhere. They may get as complex as they like. Once they have drawn a figure, ask them to arbitrarily put two points on it. Ask whether these two points are on the same side of the curve.

All plane simple closed curves share one property, no matter how complex or simple they appear. These curves divide the plane into two regions, one *inside* and the other *outside* the closed curve.

Ask students about a complicated figure. Can they tell whether two points are on the same side or different sides of the curve? To decide, students may first try to trace a path from one point to the other to see whether they need to cross any line to get to the other.

Here's an easier way. Have students draw a straight line connecting the two points. Then have them count the number of lines it intersects as it joins the points. If this number is odd, the two points are on opposite sides of the curve; if the number is even, the points are on the same side. Crossing one line gets them from outside to inside, or vice versa. Crossing a second line gets them back to the side they started from.

Here's an example of a really kooky looking curve. Points *A* and *B* are on opposite sides of the curve. The connecting line intersects three lines. If students don't believe it, have them trace a curve from *A* and see whether they get to *B* without crossing a line.

## THE GREAT CIRCULAR DIVIDE

Here is an interesting problem that will produce a design that may be used for the *Four-Color* problem. (See page 81.) What is the maximum number of regions into which a circle can be divided when any given number of straight lines are used as dividers? What is the maximum number of regions when one straight line is used? What is the number when two lines are used? When three lines are used? What about four? Can students guess the number of regions that will be generated when *any* number of lines is used?

Solutions:

| How many lines? | What does it look like? | How many regions? |
|---|---|---|
| 0 | | 1 |
| 1 | | 2 |
| 2 | | 4 |
| 3 | | 7 |
| 4 | | 11 |
| 5 | | 16 |
| 6 | | 22 |
| Any number $n$ | | $\frac{n}{2}(n+1)+1$ |

# ℕℐℳ... Type Games

Nim type games are among the most simple mathematical games to play; yet they can be played at low to high levels of sophistication. These games share certain characteristics. Two students or teams alternate turns, choosing numbers from a set, and adding (or subtracting) the numbers to form an increasing (or decreasing) sequence. The first person, or team, to bring the sequence to its goal, scores. If teams play, one member of Team A plays one member of Team B while the class looks on, and until one of the players reaches the goal and scores. The game then repeats with a new student representing each team in play.

The following are some specific games of this type.

## 3-5-7

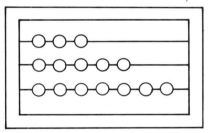

**Object:** The player to remove the last mark wins.

**Preparation:** Make three rows of chalk marks on the board: three marks in the first row, five marks in the second row, and seven marks in the third row.

**The Play:** Players take turns erasing as many marks as they like in *one row only*. They must erase at least one mark at each turn.

The following game is probably too easy for most secondary students. However, it has the same structure as '21' and may help clarify the winning strategy, which is essentially the same in both games. Use it as an introduction to '21'. If your class is enjoying this simpler game, don't hesitate to stay with it as long as interest warrants.

### '8' (Version 1)

**Object:** The first player to bring the total to 8 from its start at 0 wins.

**The Play:** Players begin at 0. They alternate, adding 1 or 2 at each turn. Keep a running total.

**Example:**

|  | Add | Total |
|---|---|---|
| **Start** |  | 0 |
| **Player A** | 1 | 1 |
| **Player B** | 2 | 3 |
| **Player A** | 2 | 5 |
| **Player B** | 1 | 6 |
| **Player A** | 2 | 8 wins! |

### '8' (Version 2)

**Object:** The first player to bring total to 0 from its start at 8 wins.

**The Play:** Players start total at 8. They alternate, subtracting 1 or 2 at each turn. Keep a running total.

**Example:**

|  | Subtract | Total |  |
|---|---|---|---|
| **Start** |  | 8 |  |
| **Player A** | 1 | 7 |  |
| **Player B** | 2 | 5 |  |
| **Player A** | 2 | 3 |  |
|  | 2 | 1 | **A subtracts 1, achieving goal of 0.** |
| **Player B loses either way** | 1 | 2 | **A subtracts 2, achieving goal of 0.** |

### '21' (Version 1)

**Object:** The first player to bring total to 21 from its start at 0, wins.

**The Play:** Players start total at 0. They take turns adding 1, 2, 3, 4, or 5 to the running total.

### '21' (Version 2)

**Object:** To bring total to 0 from its start at 21.

**Preparation:** Make twenty-one chalk marks on board.

**The Play:** Players take turns erasing 1, 2, 3, 4, or 5 marks from the board. Player who erases the last mark wins.

Math

Groups

Blackboard

Quickie

Play the entire period if it's going well, or stop to see if anyone's interested in discovering a "win-every-time" strategy. The outcome of these games can be completely determined by the first play. Who can resist the chance to know the secret of how to be a constant winner!

## Strategies

The '8' game is a good one on which to start exploring strategy because it is easy to discover the strategy in this game. After students have played for a while, they realize that the proper first move is a 2. Then, whatever number their opponent chooses, they choose the other. For example,

$$②+\boxed{1}+②+\boxed{2}+① \text{ wins.}$$

$$②+\boxed{2}+①+\boxed{1}+② \text{ wins.}$$

(Note: The moves of the player using the strategy are circled, and the opponent's are squared).

Of course, if the opponent leads with a 1, the first move would be to add 1, bringing the total to the strategic '2'.

In the '21' game, too, it is possible for the leading player always to win. Because the greatest number that may be added at one time is 5, 15 is a sure win position! An opponent can add, at most, 5 units to 15, bringing the total to 20. If the first player then adds 1, he wins.

Because 15 is a winning position, it is desirable to force the total to 15. Since $15 - 6 = 9$, 9 is also a strategic position. An opponent can add, at most, 5 units, which would bring the total to 14. The first player then adds 1 and arrives at the strategic 15. To be sure to get to 9, a player starts with 3. The largest number his opponent can add is 5, which makes $3 + 5 = 8$. The first player adds 1 to make 9, and so on. Thus, 3 is the strategic first move. The player who starts with 3 and makes no mistakes, will win the game every time!

The following are some possible games. The moves of the player using the strategy are circled, and the opponent's are squared.

$$③+\boxed{2}+④+\boxed{5}+①+\boxed{3}+③$$
$$\underbrace{\phantom{xxx}}_{6}\quad\underbrace{\phantom{xxx}}_{6}\quad\underbrace{\phantom{xxx}}_{6}$$

$$③+\boxed{5}+①+\boxed{4}+②+\boxed{2}+④$$
$$\underbrace{\phantom{xxx}}_{6}\quad\underbrace{\phantom{xxx}}_{6}\quad\underbrace{\phantom{xxx}}_{6}$$

If a player doesn't start first, he may try to get to the winning positions as follows:

$$\boxed{2}+①+$$
$$\underbrace{\phantom{xx}}_{3}$$

$$\boxed{4}+⑤+$$
$$\underbrace{\phantom{xx}}_{9=3+6}$$

$$\boxed{5}+④+$$

It is important to remember that 21 is $[(3 \times 6) + 3]$, or $(3 + 6 + 6 + 6)$.

## Developing Games and Strategy

A variation on '21' and '8' with the same strategy could be '17'. Let's permit the use of numbers 1, 2, 3, or 4. The winning first move here is 2, and the winning player completes groups of 5, because $17 = 2 + 5 + 5 + 5$. The following are some possible games:

Player has the first move:

$$②+\boxed{3}+②+\boxed{4}+①+\boxed{1}+④$$
$$\underbrace{\phantom{xx}}_{5}\quad\underbrace{\phantom{xx}}_{5}\quad\underbrace{\phantom{xx}}_{5}$$

Player doesn't have the first move:

$$\boxed{1}+①+\boxed{4}+①+\boxed{3}+②+\boxed{2}+③$$
$$\underbrace{\phantom{xx}}_{2}\quad\underbrace{\phantom{xx}}_{5}$$

$$\boxed{4}+③+\boxed{4}+①+\boxed{3}+②$$
$$\underbrace{\phantom{xx}}_{7=2+5}\quad\underbrace{\phantom{xx}}_{5}$$

88

Have students make up their own versions. They decide the total number they must reach to win and the set of numbers they may choose to add each time. Ask students to develop the winning strategy for their game.

### Strategy for 3-5-7

This strategy requires an understanding of binary notation. Don't bother with it unless you and the class are comfortable with this notation or unless you want to use the game and its strategy as motivation for learning binary notation. (We find it hard to keep that strategy in mind during play. Actually, what generally happens is you get more and more familiar with "no-win" patterns at various stages of the game. We've played 3-5-7 with third graders, and they seem to enjoy playing it. Some of the children are simply erasing, but even then, some of them *are* using strategy.) The strategy here is to force an even number of 1's in any column after each number has been expressed in base 2 notation. For example, 3 is written as 11 in base 2; 5 is written as 101 in base 2; 7 is written as 111 in base 2. Arranging these numbers in their new form, we obtain

$$
\begin{array}{r}
11 \\
101 \\
\underline{111} \\
EEO
\end{array}
$$

E means even and O means odd. We see we have an even number of 1's in the first two columns, and an odd number of 1's in the third column. A move in the winning strategy would be to reduce any number by 1, thereby making the third column even also. In this case, a proper move would be to reduce 5 to 4, which is 100 in binary notation. Thus,

$$
\begin{array}{r}
11 \\
100 \\
\underline{110} \\
EEE
\end{array}
$$

Another strategic move might be to change 7 to 6. Thus,

$$
\begin{array}{r}
11 \\
101 \\
\underline{110} \\
EEE
\end{array}
$$

This game can also be played with three heaps of counters, with any number in each heap: for example 23, 21, and 9. The strategy is the same.

# Number Games and Puzzles

## MAGIC SQUARES

**Object:** To place numbers in a tic-tac-toe grid so they form a magic square. That is, every row, column, and major (three-element) diagonal must add up to 15.

**Student Groupings:** Divide the class into two teams or into smaller groups, with several games going on simultaneously.

**Preparation:** On the blackboard, draw a tic-tac-toe grid and a list of numbers 1 through 9.

**The play:** Players take turns placing one of the nine numbers in the grid. As a number is used, it is crossed off the original list. Therefore, each number may be used only once.

**Scoring:** The first person who completes a row, column, or diagonal that does not add to 15 loses for his team. The other team scores.

Note: If you want to use the magic square as a puzzle rather than as a game, you may proceed as for Magic Triangles. A solution would be

| 2 | 9 | 4 |
|---|---|---|
| 7 | 5 | 3 |
| 6 | 1 | 8 |

The approach to a solution would be similar to that for Magic Triangles. How many number triples can you find which add up to 15? The numbers that appear three times must be placed at the corners of the grid since these corner numbers form parts of three equations (horizontal, vertical, and diagonal). For example:

| | |
|---|---|
| 1 + 9 + 5 = 15 | 2 + 7 + 6 = 15 |
| 1 + 8 + 6 = 15 | 3 + 8 + 4 = 15 |
| 2 + 9 + 4 = 15 | 3 + 7 + 5 = 15 |
| 2 + 8 + 5 = 15 | 5 + 6 + 4 = 15 |

Notice that 5 appears four times and must therefore belong at the center of the grid. The numbers 2, 8, 6, and 4 each appear three times, and must therefore belong at the corners of the grid.

## MAGIC TRIANGLES

**Object:** To arrange the first six counting numbers in a triangular figure so that the sum of the circles on each side equals 9. Later, to arrange them so they equal 10 and perhaps 11 and 12.

**Preparation:** Draw this diagram on the blackboard:

Solution:

**The play:** This may be played as a game. Follow the procedure used in Magic Squares. Another plan is to state the problem to the class. Have students work on it individually. Ask for solutions on the board.

If you need it, and the class is interested, here is a method of attacking the problem systematically: What are the possible number triples that add up to 9? For example,

$(1 + 2 + 6) = 9$
$(3 + 4 + 2) = 9$
$(1 + 5 + 3) = 9$

Which numbers appear twice? These numbers are 2, 1, 3. They must be at the corners.

## PRIME PUZZLE

**Object:** To arrange the seven prime numbers 5, 7, 11, 13, 17, 19, 23 so the rows and diagonals of the figure add to the same prime number. (A prime number is a number that is divisible only by 1 and itself.)

**Preparation:** Draw this diagram on the blackboard.

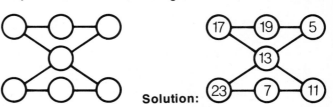

Solution:

# Palindromic Numbers

This is an excellent unit to generate addition practice!

**Object:** To transform numbers into palindromic numbers. A palindromic word, sentence, or number is one that is symmetric. It reads the same from either end. For example, *dad, deed,* and *madam* are palindromic words. *Was it a cat I saw?* is a palindromic sentence. And 7328237 and 9254774529 are palindromic numbers.

**Explanation:** Numbers that are not palindromic may be made palindromic in the following way. Reverse a number's digits, and add the original number and the reverse number together. Continue this procedure (reverse and add) until the sum is a palindromic number.

**Examples:**

|   |   |
|---|---|
| 723 | number |
| 327 | reversed |
| 1050 | added |
| 0501 | reversed |

Palindromic in two steps    1551   added

|   |   |
|---|---|
| 43 | number |
| 34 | reversed |

Palindromic in one step    77   added

|   |   |
|---|---|
| 86 | number |
| 68 | reversed |
| 154 | added |
| 451 | reversed |

Palindromic in three steps

|   |   |
|---|---|
| 605 | added |
| 506 | reversed |
| 1111 | added |

**Notes:** For all two-digit numbers in which the sum of the digits is less than 10, the first reversal and addition gives a two-digit palindrome. If the digits add to 10, 11, 12, 13, 14, 15, 16, or 18 (note that 17 is missing here), a palindrome results after 2, 1, 2, 2, 3, 4, 6, 6 reversals, respectively. If the two digits add to 17, and such a two-digit number is 89, you can see from the chart how long it takes for that number to become palindromic.

Research has shown that only 249 integers smaller than 10,000 have failed to generate a palindrome after 100 reversals. However, it has not yet been proved whether these integers will or will not become palindromic eventually.

**Procedure:** Here is a suggested list of numbers for you to have your students transform into palindromic numbers:

| Number | Number of Steps | Palindrome |
|---:|---:|---:|
| 43 | 1 | 77 |
| 723 | 2 | 1,551 |
| 86 | 3 | 1,111 |
| 94 | 2 | 484 |
| 6294 | 2 | 13,431 |
| 847 | 4 | 44,044 |
| 87 | 4 | 4,884 |
| 372 | 4 | 5,115 |
| 563 | 11 | 88,555,588 |
| 8707 | 15 | 5,233,333,325 |
| 4087 | 6 | 293,392 |
| 9479 | 7 | 9,912,199 |
| 738 | 5 | 99,099 |
| 6987 | 7 | 12,455,421 |
| 79 | 6 | 44,044 |
| 985 | 8 | 1,136,311 |
| 837 | 5 | 99,099 |
| 7084 | 6 | 293,392 |
| 4078 | 5 | 583,385 |
| 739 | 17 | 5,233,333,325 |
| 639 | 5 | 99,099 |
| 561 | 3 | 4,884 |
| 4897 | 6 | 293,392 |
| 4327 | 6 | 1,136,311 |
| 89427 | 5 | 7,296,927 |
| 489 | 3 | 9,339 |
| 95 | 3 | 1,111 |
| 589 | 8 | 1,136,311 |
| 223 | 1 | 545 |
| 89 | 24 | 8,813,200,023,188 |

Put numbers on the board as a list or one at a time. Have students make a table with headings as in the chart shown. Compare results number by number; or have the class complete a group of numbers, and score points for correct answers. Have the class make up their own numbers to investigate.

In a class discussion, ask students whether they can predict when a number will become palindromic after only one reversal. Ask students to come up with a number that is palindromic in two steps, three steps, four steps. Have the class note that some of the numbers have the same answers. Ask them to trace back why this is so.

**Reference:** An excellent reference on this subject is Martin Gardner, ''Mathematical Games: Backward Run Numbers, Letters, Words and Sentences Until Boggles the Mind,'' *Scientific American, 223,* August, 110 (1970).

# Paths, Routes,

## & Circuits

### 1

**Can you trace a path along these figures?**

—without taking your pencil from the paper
—without crossing any line
—without going over any line more than once?

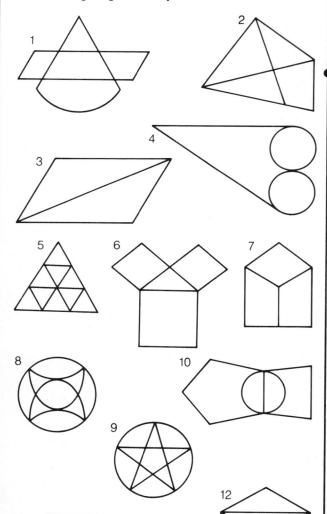

### 2

Plan the route for a complete trip around the fifteen cities of this figure. You must visit each city exactly once, returning in the end to the original home city. You may travel along any road you desire but no more than once along any road, and you may ignore any road not needed.

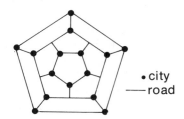

• city
— road

### 3

Can you draw a single path that crosses each edge of the figure only once and does not go through a vertex (or corner)?

An edge is a line between two vertices. A vertex looks like ● . For example Figure *a* has four vertices and five edges.

The path through Figure *b*, starting at *P* and ending at *Q*, will take you successfully through each edge.

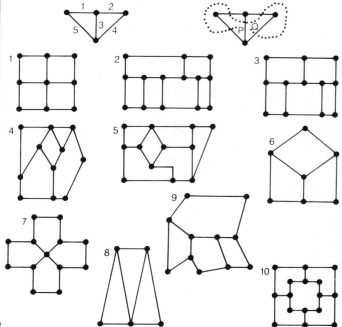

92

## Using Paths, Routes, and Circuits

Notice that this section is coded for ditto or blackboard. If you find it difficult to ditto this page before class, it is fairly simple to draw these figures on the blackboard or overhead projector. The students can copy them quite easily and proceed with the puzzles.

This page contains three different types of problems. All of them involve forming paths.

The first two problems involve tracing paths *along* lines (straight or curved) between vertices. However, the first group has the restriction that every line *must* be traced, no lines may cross, and no line may be traced more than once. In the second group because the problem is to find a route that *connects* the vertices, not all lines need be traced.

Problems of the third type (Crossing Each Edge) involve finding paths that cut the line segments between vertices. These problems involve going *in and out* of faces of figures.

Have the class make up some more of these three types of puzzles to exchange. Notice also that the diagrams for Euler lines can be used for paths crossing edges. Also, the diagrams in Crossing Each Edge can be explored to see whether they can yield Euler paths.

**Reference:** John N. Fujii, *Puzzles and Graphs,* 1966 National Council of Teachers of Mathematics, 1201 Sixteenth St., N.W., Washington, D.C. 20036.

## Trace a Path (Euler Lines)

Leonhard Euler was a great Swiss mathematician who lived from 1707 to 1783. Euler classified intersections of lines and curves as even and odd vertices. For example,

even      odd

**Discover:** If a figure has no odd vertices, it can be traced starting at any vertex. If a figure has two odd vertices, it can be traced starting at one vertex and ending at the other. If a figure has other than 0 or 2 odd vertices, it cannot be traced under the above restrictions.

The following are some solutions.

12.   5.   4.   3.   10.

## Visit Each City (Hamilton Circuit)

The solution is

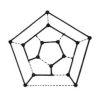

## Crossing Each Edge

A *face* of a figure refers to the region enclosed by vertices and their line segments. A face is *even* if it has an even number of lines, between vertices, enclosing it. For example,

  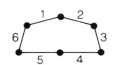

A face is *odd* if it has an odd number of lines, between vertices, enclosing it. For example,

 two odd faces          one odd face

The table shows the four situations that may arise.

| Faces   odd or even? | | Can a complete path be constructed by crossing each edge once? | Where does path start and stop? | Examples from ditto page and some solutions |
|---|---|---|---|---|
| 1. All even faces | | Yes | Start and end at same place. | 1, 5, 6, 10 |
| 2. One odd face | | Yes | Start and end at opposite sides of the odd face. | 9 |
| 3. Two odd faces | | Yes | Start inside one odd face; end inside second odd face | 2, 4 |
| 4. Three or more odd faces | | No | | 3, 7, 8 |

# Pictographs I

Connect the number pairs, and say Hello to the creature that appears! Remember, the first number of the number pair is the horizontal coordinate; the second number is the vertical coordinate.

Math
Individuals
Dittos

**A.** Number your graph paper horizontally from 0 to 28, vertically from 0 to 36.

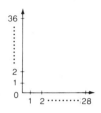

Connect these number pairs:

| | |
|---|---|
| (24, 17) | Start again. |
| (25, 11) | (9, 25) |
| (28, 20) | (8, 26) |
| (21, 24) | (8, 28) |
| (22, 26) | (11½, 31) |
| (22, 33) | (16, 29) |
| (20, 36) | (18, 31) |
| (19, 34) | (20, 31) |
| (8, 32) | (21½, 29) |
| (6, 34) | (21½, 27) |
| (4, 24) | (21, 26) |
| (1, 22) | |

(1, 7)   Draw eyes
(10, 18)   that look like 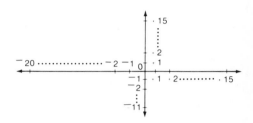 and are centered
(6, 23)   at (11½, 26½) and
(8, 24)   (18½, 27).
(14, 23)
(17, 21)
(19, 24)
(21, 24)
(24, 17)
(18, 6)
(19, 2)
(16, 5)
(13, 5)
(10, 1)
(10, 5)
(6, 13)
(3, 3)
(8, 3)
(9, 7)
STOP!

**B.** Number your graph paper horizontally from 0 to 23 vertically from 0 to 37.

Connect these number pairs:

| | |
|---|---|
| (4, 26) | Start again: |
| (3, 23) | (8, 24) |
| (4, 22) | (6, 22) |
| (6, 22) | (9, 24) |
| (6, 19) | (9, 26) |
| (3, 16) | (7, 26) |
| (3, 12) | (6, 27) |
| (9, 15) | (5, 27) |
| (9, 12) | (4, 26) |
| (10, 12½) | (3½, 25) |
| (12, 8) | (2, 27) |
| (15, 6) | (3, 30) |
| (18, 6) | (1, 31) |
| (16, 2) | (2, 33) |
| (20, 2) | (4, 34) |
| (22, 8) | (5, 33) |
| (22, 16) | (10, 33) |
| (20, 15) | (9, 35) |
| (19, 14) | (12, 36) |
| (17, 10) | (13, 35) |
| (18, 6) | (14, 33) |
| STOP! | (13, 32) |
| | (17, 30) |
| Start again: | (19, 25) |
| Connect: | (21, 22) |
| (21, 20) and | (21, 20) |
| (22, 16) | (20, 19) |
| | (19, 16) |
| | (14, 14) |
| | (9, 12) |
| | (8, 10) |
| | (10, 7) |
| | (7, 3) |
| | (14, 4) |
| | (15, 6) |
| | STOP! |

You're all done now, except you'll need some eyes. Draw them to look like 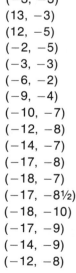 with points P at (4, 27) and (7½, 27).

**C.** This one is on four quadrants. Number your graph paper as shown in this diagram:

Connect these number pairs:

(5, −1)
(13, −1)
(5, 12)
(5, −3)
(4, −3)
(4, 8)
(−2, −2)
(4, −2)
STOP!

Start again:
(−3, −3)
(13, −3)
(12, −5)
(−2, −5)
(−3, −3)
(−6, −2)
(−9, −4)
(−10, −7)
(−12, −8)
(−14, −7)
(−17, −8)
(−18, −7)
(−17, −8½)
(−18, −10)
(−17, −9)
(−14, −9)
(−12, −8)

Now make tiny circles around these six points:
(−13, −8)
(−12, −7)
(−12, −6)
(−12, −5)
(−13, −4)
(−14, −3)

That's it!

# Pictographs II

Connect the number pairs and see what appears! Remember, the first number of the number pair is the horizontal coordinate; the second number is the vertical coordinate.

**A.** This fellow is in all four quadrants. Number your paper as shown in this diagram.

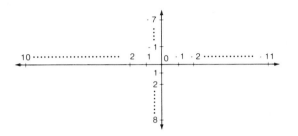

Connect these number pairs:

| | | |
|---|---|---|
| (−5, 2) | (8, −1) | Start again: |
| (−6, 2) | (8, 1) | (3, 0) |
| (−8, 1) | (7, 3) | (3, −2) |
| (−7, 0) | (6, 4) | (4, −3) |
| (−8, −2) | (3, 5) | (5, −3½) |
| (−9, −2) | (−2, 4) | |
| (−9, −3) | (−5, 2) | Now you're almost finished; put a tiny eye, like this, ◉ centered at (−6, −1). |
| (−4, −5) | (−4, 2) | |
| (−4, −6) | (−3, 1) | And add his tail. |
| (−5, −7) | (−4, 0) | |
| (−4, −7) | (−5, 0) | (8, 1) |
| (−3, −6) | (−6, 1) | (10, 1) |
| (−3, −5) | (−7, 1) | (10, 2) |
| (−2, −5) | STOP! | (9, 2) |
| (−2, −6) | | (9, 1) |
| (−3, −7) | Start again: | (10, 0) |
| (−2, −7) | (−3, −3) | |
| (−1, −6) | (−3, −4) | |
| (−1, −5) | (−2, −5) | |
| (4, −4) | STOP! | |

(4, −5)
(3, −6)
(4, −6)
(5, −5)
(5, −3½)
(6, −4)
(6, −6)
(5, −7)
(6, −7)
(7, −6)
(7, −5)
(8, −4)
(7, −3)
(7, −2)
Continue above

**B.** Number your graph paper horizontally from 0 to 30 vertically from 0 to 38.

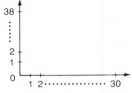

Connect these number pairs:

| | | |
|---|---|---|
| (20, 35) | (10, 15) | Start again: |
| (19, 34) | (8, 14) | (17, 13) |
| (20, 33) | (6, 13) | (16, 10) |
| (20, 32) | STOP! | (20, 10) |
| (24, 32) | | (24, 9) |
| (27, 33) | Start again: | (28, 9) |
| (29, 32) | (19, 20) | STOP! |
| (27, 36) | (18, 18) | |
| (23, 36) | (17, 17) | Start again: |
| (20, 35) | (15, 16) | (23, 6) |
| (17, 37) | (12, 15) | (23, 7) |
| (14, 35) | (10, 13) | (24, 9) |
| (13, 31) | (7, 9) | (26, 11) |
| (17, 24) | (10, 6) | (27, 11) |
| (16, 22) | (12, 3) | STOP! |
| (11, 24) | (14, 3) | |
| (5, 21) | (15, 1) | Start again: |
| (1, 23) | STOP! | (24, 9) |
| (2, 19) | | (26, 10) |
| (1, 17) | Start again: | (28, 10) |
| (4, 18) | (9, 1) | STOP! |
| (3, 16) | (10, 2) | |
| (5, 17) | (12, 3) | You're finished, except for an eye ◉ at (18½, 34). |
| (6, 13) | (14, 5) | |
| (3, 13) | (16, 4) | |
| (6, 12) | STOP! | |
| (10, 13) | | |
| (17, 13) | Start again: | |
| (23, 16) | (12, 3) | |
| (18, 30) | (14, 4) | |
| (20, 32) | (16, 3) | |
| (20, 33) | STOP! | |
| (23, 34) | | |
| (26, 34) | | |
| (27, 33) | | |

STOP!

Continue here:
(14, 20)
(12, 19)
and onto the next column.

**Answers to Pictograph**

**Solution to Pictograph I A**

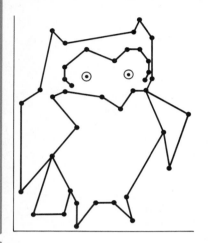

**Solution to Pictograph I B**

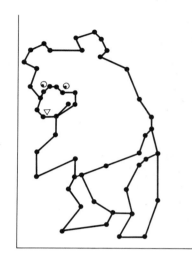

**Solution to Pictograph I C**

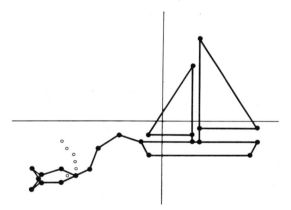

**Solution to Pictograph II A**

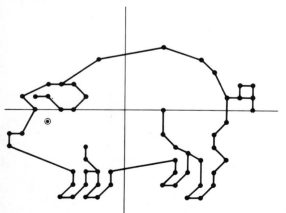

**Solution to Pictograph II B**

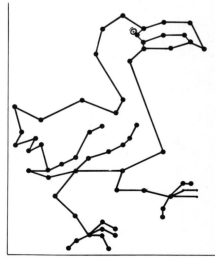

# POLYOMINOES

This is an exploration in combinatorial geometry, which deals with ways in which geometric shapes can be combined. Polyominoes are configurations formed by joining congruent squares along their edges.

### Correct joining of two squares (joined along edge)
### Incorrect joining of two squares (joined only at vertex)

Discover with the class how many different figures can be formed by joining a particular number of squares. Students may take turns, at the board, drawing their solutions.

Have students discover how many different forms of each figure there are. Here we define two figures as different when one cannot cover the other, even when it is rotated or flipped. We define *domino* as the figure formed by joining two squares. How many different dominoes are there? There is only one. Note that

is the same as

because the first will cover the second when rotated. We define *tromino* as the figure formed by joining three squares. There are two different trominoes.

the straight tromino        the right tromino

We define *tetromino* as the figure formed by joining four squares. Let the class discover that there are five different tetrominoes. If students think they have discovered more, have them keep rotating or flipping, and they will find that one is congruent to another.

straight        square        left

T        skew

We define *pentomino* as the figure formed by joining five squares. Let the class discover that there are twelve distinct combinations.

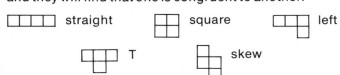

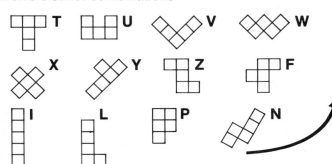

## Puzzle

Can *all* the pentominoes (5-□'s) be made using any tromino (3-□) and the domino (2-□)? Restriction: Tromino and domino must be used intact. They may not be cut into individual squares. Answer: All but one can; X is the exception.

## Symmetries

As your students discover the possible shapes, you might ask them to consider which pieces have *fold symmetry;* that is, which pieces may be folded along a line such that the two halves are congruent. Have students discover how many of each type (3-□, 4-□, 5-□, etc.) have this property.

## Game

Draw a 5 by 5 matrix on the blackboard.

**Object:** To fill the board with 3-squares. Last player to place a 3-square wins.

**Student groupings:** Two teams. Two players (one from each team) alternate placing pieces until one wins. Then two others play.

**Materials:** Two colors of chalk.

**The play:** Players using different colored chalk take turns filling in 3-squares as though they were covering them with a tromino. Remember, there are two shapes possible (        and        ).

**Example:** After four plays, the board might look like this:

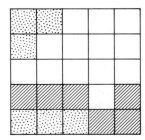

The last player able to place a piece (color the squares) wins.

A *hexomino* is the figure formed by joining six squares. Let the class discover that there are thirty-five distinct hexominoes.

The twenty-four *odd* hexominoes will cover an odd number of light and dark squares if laid on a checkerboard.

97

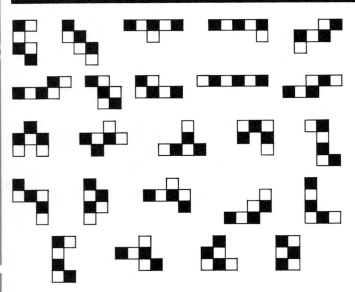

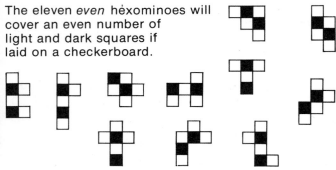

The eleven *even* hexominoes will cover an even number of light and dark squares if laid on a checkerboard.

Explore which shapes are even hexominoes and which shapes are odd hexominoes.

To summarize, so far, there are

| | |
|---|---|
| 1 distinct | domino 2-□ |
| 2 distinct | trominoes 3-□ |
| 5 distinct | tetrominoes 4-□ |
| 12 distinct | pentominoes 5-□ |
| 35 distinct | hexominoes 6-□ |
| 108 distinct | heptominoes 7-□ including |

including the controversial ↗ with its interior hole.

## Extending the Idea

Explore the possibilities for combining congruent equilateral triangles in the same way that we did congruent squares. How many ways can students combine different numbers of triangles? The joining principle remains the same as before. Triangles may properly be joined only along an edge. Have students look at

three equilateral triangles. These can be joined in only one way:

If students think they have discovered another way, they will find it will cover this figure if they rotate it.

Have students combine four equilateral triangles in as many ways as they can. Starting with the only possible arrangement for three triangles, they add a fourth triangle along the edges of this figure. They will obtain

The other possibilities, for example,

are the same as *b* under a flip. Similarly,

is the same as *c* under a flip. Continue this exploration as you did with the squares. (See solutions below).

It may be fun to have students compare the number of ways the square figures can be arranged with the number of possibilities for the triangular figures. There seem to be more square figures generated than triangular ones for any number of figures greater than two. Ask students whether they think this has anything to do with the fact that a square has more sides to add onto than a triangle.

**Solutions:**

| How many triangles? | How many ways? |
|:---:|:---:|
| 2 | 1 |
| 3 | 1 |
| 4 | 3 |
| 5 | 4 |
| 6 | 12 |
| 7 | 24 |

**Reference:** An excellent reference on this subject by the man who introduced it to puzzle fans and invented many of the problems presented here is *Polyominoes* by Solomon W. Golomb, (George Allen & Unwin Ltd. London, 1966)

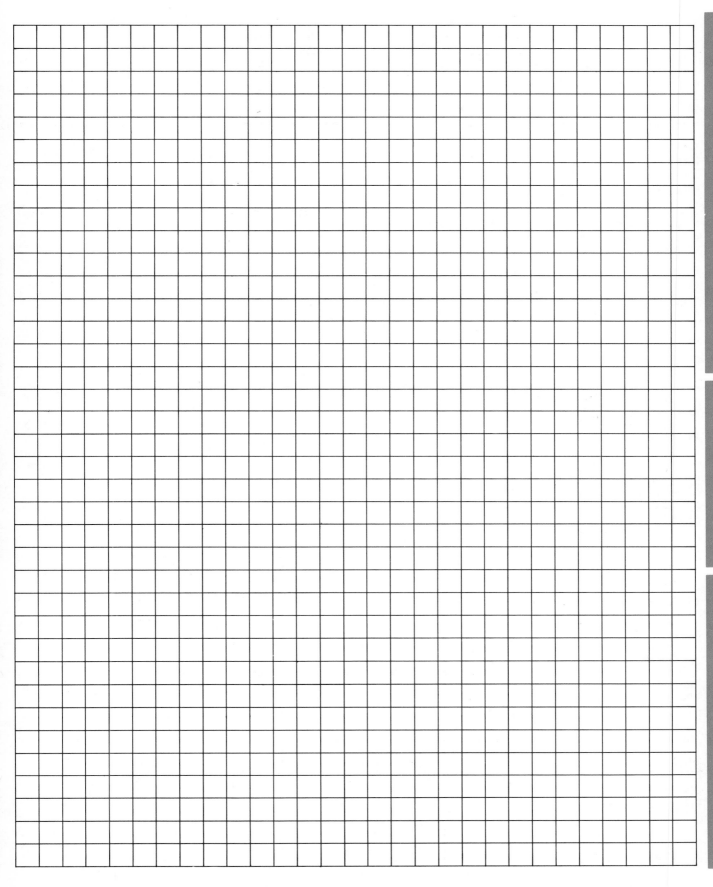

# COMPARE THE PAIR

Science

Individuals Groups Class

Other Blackboard

**Object:** To observe, through experiment, how students interpret the meaning of the word *compare*. Does *compare* mean to look at differences or does it mean to look at similarities?

Don't discuss the object of this experiment beforehand. Such discussion will make the student's reactions self-conscious, and will weaken the validity of the experiment.

**Preparation:** Place two different objects in a convenient place, in clear sight of the class. Possibilities might be a book and a blackboard eraser, a stapler and a ruler, a stapler and a book, a thumb tack and a paper clip, or a book and a wastepaper basket. Have the class suggest other objects in the room.

(For our suggestions, we've mentioned items that are most certain to be found in any classroom. Remember though, *any* two different objects will do. The more dramatically different they are, the easier it will be to make the comparisons.)

**Procedure:** Have students, working individually, compare the two objects they see and list as many points of comparison between them as they can. After this has been done, divide the class into sections of three to four students each. Ask the individuals in each group to pool their lists of comparisons. Have each group compile data from its composite list after you have read the following questions aloud, written them on the board, or preferably done both.

1. What was the total number of comparisons recorded?

2. (a) How many items referred to **similarities** between the two objects?

(b) What percentage of all the items were these similarities?

3. (a) How many items referred to **differences** between the two objects?
   (b) What percentage of all the items were these differences?

4. How many of the items of comparison referred to shape or form? This includes reference to relative position on the display area (desk or whatever)

5. How many of the items were a comparison of the use or function of the objects?

6. How many items were a comparison of size?

7. How many items were a comparison of material?

8. How many items were a comparison of color?

9. How many items were a comparison of distinctive or functional markings?

While each group is collecting this information, on the board prepare a matrix that will gather all this information together. It might be a mapping of the different student groups (for example, A, B, C, etc.) versus the numbers of the questions. See matrix.

Have members of each team come to the board to record their data.

Have students compare 2(b) with 3(b). Which is greater? Do all the groups show 3(b) greater than 2(b)? Are these results surprising? Among items 4 through 9, which are compared most often? Least often? What other conclusions can you draw from this chart?

| Group | 1 Total | 2(a) similarities | 2(b) Percentage Similarities | 3(a) Differences | 3(b) Percentage Differences | 4 Shape Form | 5 Use | 6 Size | 7 Material | 8 Color | 9 Marks |
|---|---|---|---|---|---|---|---|---|---|---|---|
| A | | | | | | | | | | | |
| B | | | | | | | | | | | |
| C | | | | | | | | | | | |
| D ⋮ | | | | | | | | | | | |
| Total | | | | | | | | | | | |

# ESP Fact or Fantasy

Some forty years ago, four members of the psychology department of Duke University decided to study telepathy and clairvoyance as laboratory research problems. Thus was born the field of parapsychology. While scientists agree that people obtain information through the use of their senses, parapsychologists believe that information is obtained in additional ways. They experiment to explore the hypothesis that the mind obtains some kinds of information in ways that cannot be explained by the use of any known senses. They postulate another form of perception which they call extrasensory perception, or ESP. Professor Joseph Banks Rhine of Duke University and others believe the existence of some kinds of ESP has been scientifically proved. Others believe it has not yet been proved. Critics of ESP experiments claim that the experimental procedures are not sufficiently controlled to produce valid results. It is not usually possible for skeptical observers to repeat results. Believers claim ESP is a delicate force, which only works when explored by sympathetic observers on sympathetic subjects. One indisputable statement can be made however. No one has yet proved that ESP does *not* exist.

## Vocabulary

**ESP (extrasensory perception)**—perception not based on normal use of the senses. A term coined by Joseph Banks Rhine, designating awareness of or response to objects, events (clairvoyance), or another person's thoughts (telepathy) without the mediation of the senses.

**clairvoyance**—a form of ESP in which there is awareness of or response to objects or events without the mediation of the senses. A kind of *seeing without eyes.*

**telepathy**—thought transference, "mind reading." A form of ESP in which there is awareness of or response to another person's thoughts without the mediation of the senses.

**precognition**—knowledge of events before they happen in time. ESP directed to future events or thoughts. A kind of *hunch.*

**PK (psychokinesis)**—an alleged direct influence exerted by a person on a physical system without the use of any known form of physical energy (for example, causing objects to move by willing it).

**psychologist**—one who studies the human mind and individual behavior.

**parapsychologist**—one who studies mental phenomena for which no physical cause can be found. The study of phenomena such as ESP, ghosts, mediums, which are disclaimed or ignored by orthodox psychologists.

## An Experiment

The following is a classic experiment of the type Professor Rhine has used to explore the existence of ESP. Try it with your class. First, define ESP. Ask students whether they have heard of it and what they think about it. Perhaps explore the vocabulary together.

**Materials:** Bring a set of blank cards to class. You will want a few more than one card per student. The size of the cards is not important, but they should be of uniform size. Small index cards, for example, will be fine. If there is a paper cutter around, you might cut some 3 by 5 cards into 3 by 2½, or you might be able to cut up some tagboard. Or you can make do with paper that has been cut or torn into unit sizes (perhaps by the students in the class). Remember, though, that you want to perform the experiment with cards that are as opaque as possible.

**Preparation:**
1. Pass out the cards to the class, one card to each student. While this is being done, draw a five-card set of ESP cards on the board. They look like this:

| plus | three parallel wavy lines | circle | square or rectangle | five-point star |

2. Because you will need twenty-five cards for the experiment (five each of the five designs), ask each student to draw one of the five designs on his card. If you have at least five rows in your class, the students in each row may draw one particular design; that is, all the students in the first row would put a plus on their cards, those in the second row the parallel wavy lines, etc. Encourage the students to cooperate with one another, because their symbols should be as alike as possible in size, thickness, and shape. When the students have completed their cards (one each), have someone collect the cards and compile an ESP deck, made up of twenty-five cards, five each of five designs.

**3.** Ask each student to make a chart of the five designs on a piece of paper. It should look like this:

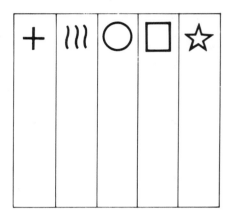

*Before you begin the experiment, you may want to insert a minilesson on probability. Does everyone realize that if we have five different designs, the chance of calling the correct card, without seeing it, is one out of five? That means the number of correct card symbols one is likely to call, by chance, is two out of ten, three out of fifteen, five out of twenty-five, etc. In a very large number of runs, these are the scores that chance would tend toward. In the size run you are likely to have time for, as many as eight out of twenty-five correct guesses would not yet be significant. Any score higher than this however would be attributed, by certain investigators, to extra sensory perception (ESP). For example, a subject who consistently calls nine correct responses out of twenty-five would be considered an ESP-sensitive subject. Notice we underline "consistently." These numbers would have to repeat several times to be significant. Encourage the class to explore this idea.*

**Procedure:** Choose two students from the class to work out of sight of the others. (Use your ingenuity here. Put the card handlers in the back of the room; improvise a barrier with a screen; have them work down on the floor behind the teacher's desk; or look for a closet large enough and light enough for them to work in.) One student turns up the cards, one at a time. The second student makes a list of the designs as they appear. One fast way he may record this information is to head a sheet of paper with the five designs and write the numerals referring to first card observed, second card, third card, and so on under each design. For example, if the cards are turned up in this order,

$$+, \text{///}, +, \bigcirc, \square, \bigcirc, \bigcirc, \cdots$$

the chart will look like this:

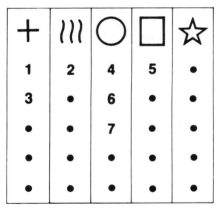

While this is happening, the remaining students in the class are recording their guesses, in the same way, on their charts. It may be useful to have a third person (perhaps you) calling first card, second card, and so on as the cards are turned up. This helps keep track of the number to associate with a particular card guess, and students do not obtain any vocal clues from the person who is turning up the cards or the one who is seeing them and recording the actual correct order.

**Evaluate the data:** Have the students exchange papers or score their own. The student who has been keeping track of the correct sequence of cards calls the sequence aloud as follows: 1, plus; 2, wavy line; 3, plus; 4, circle; 5, square; 6, circle, etc. The students evaluating their papers need only mark correct responses, perhaps by putting a large check through them or circling them. Now all that is needed is to total the number of correct responses.

Look at the data from the entire class. Is anyone ESP-sensitive? That is, does anyone have nine or more correct guesses out of the twenty-five? You may ask for the correct numbers for each student. Post these on the board.

Do at least one more run, and a few more if you have time. (Remember to re-shuffle the cards each time). Do particular people seem to do consistently better than chance in their scores? Rhine says that one in five subjects has ESP powers. If you have time, you might try to test these people separately.

## Another test

A test for *precognition* is to have each student choose the order of twenty-five cards as he wishes; that is, he should assign numerals from one to twenty-five to the designs on his chart. Then have someone shuffle the cards to establish their order. Students could then check their papers as someone calls off the order of the cards. Again, score correct responses, and look for ESP-sensitives! (Notice here that the order is reversed: First guess the cards; then shuffle and establish their order.)

**Note:** There are three distinct experiments for testing different kinds of ESP powers.

Testing for *telepathy* was done in the first experiment. One student sees each card as it is turned up. He may conceivably be telepathically sending a message that a sensitive subject may be picking up.

In a test for *clairvoyance,* the deck is shuffled first. Students try to determine the order of the deck after it is established. The only way in which this differs from telepathy is that no one has seen the cards and thus cannot be sending telepathic messages. In the telepathy experiment, one student sees each card as it

is turned up. In a clairvoyance test, no one sees the cards until after the subject has recorded his guess. If the subject scores higher than chance in such a test, some researchers would claim that the subject has clairvoyant powers, which enable him to obtain the information without the use of his ordinary senses.

The test for *precognition* has been described above. Students first guess the order of the cards on their charts. Then the deck is shuffled, and the order of the cards is established.

# Experiment with Pulse, Breath, Hands, and Eyes

Here is a series of experiments you may have fun doing with your students. Your students bring into the classroom all the equipment they will need to do these experiments—pulse, breath, hands, eyes. There are five experiments in this section. They use the essentials of the experimental method—observation, recording of data, analysis of results, and conclusions. Each is completely independent. Depending on how much attention you give to the analysis of the data, they may require short or long periods of time. Explore them as time and interest permits.

## Explore Hand folding

**Problem:** When hands are folded, does the right hand thumb cross over the left hand thumb, or does the left hand thumb cross over the right hand thumb?

**Procedure:** Have students clasp hands at a given signal. Repeat two or three times. Observe results. (Each student will probably find the same result each time.)

**Analysis:** Collect the data for the entire class. How many students find their thumbs cross right over left? Call this R o L. How many students find their thumbs cross left over right? Call this L o R. Make a matrix on the blackboard. This is a fine way to consolidate information. It might look like this:

|  | R o L | L o R |
|---|---|---|
| Boys | 1 | 3 |
| Girls | 2 | 4 |

*If you've forgotten how to fill in matrix: In square 1, place the number of boys who fold right over left. In square 2, place the number of girls who fold right over left. In square 3, place the number of boys who fold left over right. In square 4, place the number of girls who fold left over right.*

Explore whether there is any correlation between this property and right- or left-handedness. Perhaps expand the matrix as follows:

|  | R H | | L H | |
|---|---|---|---|---|
|  | R o L | L o R | R o L | L o R |
| Boys | 1 | 3 | 5 | 7 |
| Girls | 2 | 4 | 6 | 8 |

Look into the number of people who are R o L and R. H., R o L and L. H., L o R and L. H., or L o R and R. H.

## Explore Right-eyed and Left-eyed

**Problem:** In the same way that people are right-handed and left-handed, they may also be characterized as right-eyed and left-eyed.

**Procedure:** Ask students to use both eyes and point their right index finger at some object all the students can see. Then, while they continue to point at the object with their right index finger, ask them to close their right eye. If the object appears to shift to the right, they are considered right-eyed. If the object does not appear to shift at all, they are considered left-eyed.

This data may *also* be gathered in a matrix in various ways, and it may also be added to an expanded matrix above: This would be an interesting way to look for any correlations between right- and left-handedness and eyedness.

*The next three experiments require a clock or watch for measuring rates. The rates we are measuring are pulse rates, breathing rates (perhaps with attention to correlations between them), and blinking rates. In the analyses, we will use some of the ideas of statistics. We will calculate averages, medians, modes, and ranges.*

Average: *total of all the individual rates divided by the number of students.*

Median: *the rate which is in the middle of the list if all the rates in the class are listed in order according to size (from smallest to largest, or visa versa).*

Mode: *the rate which appears most frequently on the list.*

Range: *the difference between the smallest rate and the greatest rate.*

*If a sample collection of data is 7, 8, 8, 10, 11, 12, 14, the average value is*

$$\frac{7 + 8 + 8 + 10 + 11 + 12 + 14}{7} = \frac{70}{7} = 10$$

*The median value is 10. The mode is 8. The range is 14 − 7 = 7.*

## Explore Blinking Rate

**Student Groupings:** Groups of three students each. One student is the subject. One student is the observer. One student is the timekeeper.

**Procedure:** Observe the number of times the subject blinks his eyes within a given interval of time, perhaps two minutes. Students reverse roles until the rates are established for each member of the trio. Collect the rates for all the students in the class.

**Analysis:** What are the statistics for this experiment? What is the average blink rate for the class? What is the median? What is the mode? What is the range?

## Explore Pulse Rate

**Student Groupings:** Groups of two students each. One student is the subject. The second student senses and records the pulse rate.

**Procedure:** Students should first practice finding the pulse. Students will find that the pulse is on the palm side of the wrist, on an approximately straight line down from the thumb. Have them lightly rest the first, second and third fingers of the hand on the pulse, while the thumb rests on the side of the wrist behind the palm. Be sure they don't use the thumb when sensing the pulse since the thumb has a slight pulse of its own, and this may confuse the results. When you find that they can locate the pulse easily you are ready to start.

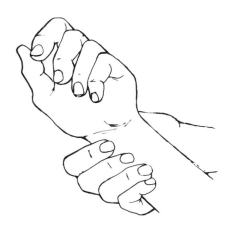

Pick a time interval, one minute perhaps. Count the number of pulse beats in that length of time. Record the data.

**Analysis:** Combine the data for the class and look at the various statistics, as in the previous experiment. You may separate the data for boys and girls and see whether there are any significant differences. If interest warrants, look at what happens to pulse rate under conditions of physical exertion. For example, have the subject jump in position for a given number of times. It is necessary to be fairly good at locating the pulse to get the value of this variation. We have found that the pulse rate is certainly much speeded up as a result of such activity, but it tends to settle back to normal fairly quickly. If students fumble locating the pulse, they tend to miss most of the variation. However, if the class is interested, it is worth exploring the difference.

## Explore Breathing Rate

**Student groupings:** By Individuals. Here everyone can probably best keep track of his own rate while one person keeps track of the time for the entire class.

**Procedure:** At a given time, have students start counting how many breaths they take. You call a halt after some interval, say two minutes. Everyone records the number of breaths they have taken.

**Analysis:** Look at the experimental statistics for the class—the range of rates, and so on.

# EXPLORE LEARNING

Here is a series of experiments that may serve to give insight into the mechanisms of learning, and the roles played by *habit, sense versus nonsense,* and *trial and error* in learning.

## Habit (Experiment 1)

Here is an experiment that will dramatize the power of habit. Habits are time savers. Tasks utilizing habit require little conscious thought.

**Student groupings:** Individuals or preferably in pairs.

**Procedure:** Have students write their full name as many times as they are able to do so in a given length of time (for example, half a minute.) Then ask them to write their name with their *other* hand as many times as they can in the same time interval. Let each non-writing partner keep track of the time for the writing partner.

**Analysis:** Have students record the number of times they have written the name under each circumstance. Ask what causes the difference.

## Habit (Experiment 2)

**Student groupings:** By individuals. Teacher or particular student dictates to class.

**Procedure:** Pick a passage from a book to dictate to the class. If everybody has a textbook, pick a paragraph from it in order that students may follow the dictation. The students are to write the material as it is read to them. Don't worry about spelling. The experiment is not concerned with that. Keep track of the time. Read at a comfortable rate.

Do this a second time, but add one change in direction. Ask the students to write as you dictate—only this time they are not to cross any *t*'s or dot any *i*'s. Have students score how many dotted *i*'s and crossed *t*'s they have accidentally made. If you want to take the time, it might be interesting to repeat this experiment several times and record the rate of relearning. That is, how many dotted *i*'s and crossed *t*'s appear in successive trials. Have each student keep track of his own results.

Make a graph on the blackboard which shows the class results. Here you would graph the number of students versus the number of dotted *i*'s. On the same graph, you might graph the number of students versus the number of crossed *t*'s. You would now have two curves plotted on the same graph.

You might prefer to gather the data on two separate graphs, one for recording dotted *i*'s and the other recording crossed *t*'s. Of course, this would mainly be of interest if you repeat the experiment several times. Each curve would then show the successive results. This would be a graphic way to record the progress of learning when the learning involves undoing habit.

## Sense versus Nonsense

(See also *Memory Dial,* page 42.)

**Student groupings:** The class together.

**Procedure:** Choose a well-known saying. For example, you might pick "A stitch in time saves nine." You might ask students to suggest well-known sayings by handing them to you on folded sheets of paper. Write the saying on the board in two columns. Column A shows the words jumbled. Column B shows the words in order. (Try to figure out a way to keep what you have written hidden so everyone sees it for the first time at the same time. An overhead projector works very well here.) The columns might look like this:

| Column A | Column B |
|----------|----------|
| in | a |
| saves | stitch |
| nine | in |
| time | time |
| stitch | saves |
| a | nine |

Now uncover Column A. Ask the students to memorize the words in order. Have them raise their hands when they have memorized the words. Have two students keep score on the board. The data you record is the time that has elapsed and the name of the student. Allow this to go on for about five minutes. How many students feel they have achieved the task? How many students feel they have memorized the nonsense list of words?

Uncover Column B. (This is the column that makes sense.) Ask the students to memorize these words in order. Record how many students have memorized this list in twenty seconds, thirty seconds, etc.

**Analysis:** Why was Column B so much easier to memorize than Column A? What does this tell students about learning in general?

## Trial and Error

Trial and error is one of the most time-consuming ways to learn.

**Materials:** Four pieces of paper or card, each of the following shape; each student has his own four pieces.

This is the piece to be cut out.

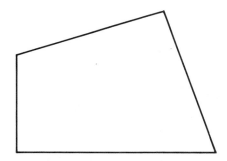

*You can do this experiment only if you can make a fast ditto of this shape to bring into the class or if you can cut four to eight of these shapes out of card and pass these around for the students to use as a template.*

*Each student should make four copies of this shape. They must be exactly the same.*

*If scissors are available, they can be cut out easily. However, if scissors are not available, secondary students should be able to tear them successfully by folding back and forth along the edge to be cut. This will be fairly easy if you take advan-*

*tage of the corner right angles of an ordinary sheet of paper. Because the figure has two right angles, each of the four pieces to be cut may best be laid out at the corners of a sheet of paper. In this way, it will be necessary only to cut or tear two edges for each figure rather than four.*

This is called a Dissection Puzzle. Here is the solution to this one.

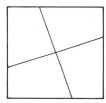

**Procedure and Analysis:** At a given signal, the students are to put their four pieces together to form a perfect square. Each student may raise his hand when he has successfully completed his puzzle. (One student might keep a written record on the board of names and times of completion of the different students.)

Have the successful students put their pieces away for five minutes and then try to do the puzzle again. How long does it take them to put it together the second time?

Are there some students who were successful once and can't repeat their success? What does this mean? (Hit-and-miss learning is unreliable.)

If a student in the class has been very successful with the puzzle, see whether he can explain his system to the class in great detail. (He probably had some plan in mind if he was repeatedly successful. Did he try to make two symmetric halves and then combine them? Did he realize he must put a right angle in the corner because the corner angles of a square are right angles? Did he locate the right angles in the puzzle pieces?)

After the student has shared his method with the class, you might have the class again try to put their puzzle together, all starting at the same time. Record the results this time. How do they compare with previous results?

# FINGERISTICS
## Observations and Relations

**Problem:** How do the lengths of an individual's fingers vary? Is the index finger (finger 1) longer than the ring finger (finger 3)? Is the opposite the case? How does the order of lengths of an individual's fingers compare with his neighbor's fingers? What does the class "finger profile" look like?

**Procedure:** Have each student place his left hand, palm down, fingers slightly spread, on a sheet of paper. The student should now carefully draw around the outline of the fingers of the hand. He should mark the fingers on the outline as shown. (Make certain here that all the students number their fingers in the same way. Otherwise, the data will be nonsense).

Order finger numbers according to length, from longest to shortest. For example, according to the diagram, the results show that finger 2 is longest; finger 3 is second longest; 4 and 1 are the same (third longest); and the thumb is fourth longest. There may be some disagreement about precisely how to measure finger length. See whether the class can come up with a measuring method on which all can agree.

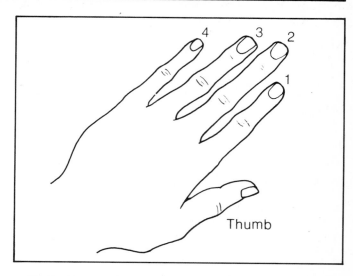

While the students are making their outlines and ordering their finger lengths, make a chart or matrix on the board. The matrix might look like this:

| Number of Students | Longest Finger | Second Longest Finger | Third Longest Finger | Fourth Longest Finger | Fifth Longest Finger |
|---|---|---|---|---|---|
| ? | 2 | 3 | 1 | 4 | thumb |
| ? | 2 | 3 | 1 | thumb | 4 |
| ? | 2 | 1 and 3 same | thumb and 4 same | — | — |
| ? | 1, 2, 3 same | thumb | 4 | — | — |
| ? | 2 | 1 | 3 | thumb | 4 |
| etc. | | | | | |

When the students have recorded their results, you might proceed as follows: "Raise your hand if your second finger length is longest, third next longest, and so on, (as indicated along the first line of the matrix)." Record the number of students whose finger lengths were ordered in this way. "Raise your hand if the information is the same as on the second line of the matrix." Record the number of raised hands under number of students in the first column and second line. Continue this procedure through the listed combinations. Are there any cases different from those already appearing on the board? Ask the class to offer any other orders they have found. Remember to ask for *numbers* of students for each new ordering of finger lengths.

Have students look at the matrix. How many students had their second finger longest? How many students had their third finger longest? How many students had two fingers the same length? How many students had two pairs of fingers the same length? Is there time to break the data into girls versus boys?

Until now we have been determining the lengths of the fingers by measuring them from stem to tip. How does the order of lengths we have found this way compare with the order we find if we look at our fingers another way? Have students press their fingers together and consider their comparative lengths as the distance between the tips of the fingers and a reference line. This reference might be a straight line drawn perpendicular to the longest finger. For this example, it is probably safe to say that the thumb is always the shortest finger because it is the one furthest from the reference line.

Ask students to check the lengths and orderings of fingers of parents and siblings. Is this ordering a genetic function?

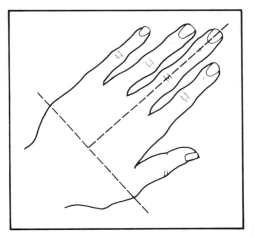

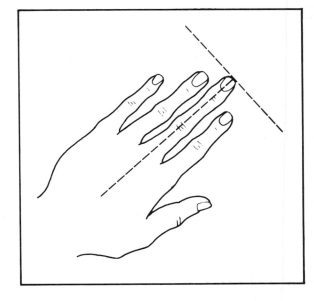

# FINGERPRINTS!

## A study in arches, loops and whorls

whorl    loop    arch

**A Bit of History** * *

Interest in modern fingerprint identification dates from 1880 when two Englishmen, Henry Faulds and William James Hesschel, published papers on the subject. They described the uniqueness and permanence of fingerprints. Sir Frances Galton, an English scientist, soon verified their findings, and his research indicated that identical fingerprints were not inherited. His elementary classification system was later extended by Sir Edward R. Henry, chief commissioner of the London metropolitan police. The Henry system of fingerprint classification was introduced at Scotland Yard in 1901 and is the basis of an extended system of filing used by the Federal Bureau of Investigation (FBI) today.

You will need a piece of carbon paper, ink pads, or a washable felt tip pen.

Practice getting a good fingerprint. By a good print, we mean one clear enough so you can identify the markings as arch, loop, or whorl. When you feel you can get a fairly good print, put prints of your ten fingers in the appropriate squares of the chart. Put your name on your set of prints.

In the spaces below the squares, print and classify the print of each finger as arch, loop, or whorl. Here it may be useful to work in groups of two or three. Sometimes it is *hard to decide* whether a print is an arch or a loop or a whorl. Look carefully!

*Carbon paper works very well. The best way to get the required amount of ink on the finger is to rub the pad of your finger back and forth (laterally) on the carbon side of the carbon paper. Also, the slicker the paper the print is on, the clearer the impression and the easier it is to read.*

| **Example:**  Loop | 1. Right thumb | 2. Right index | 3. Right middle | 4. Right ring | 5. Right little |
|---|---|---|---|---|---|
| Pattern type | | | | | |
| | 6. Left thumb | 7. Left index | 8. Left middle | 9. Left ring | 10. Left little |
| | | | | | |
| Pattern type | | | | | |

Social Studies   Science   Math

Individuals   Groups

Dittos*

Other

## Using Fingerprints

This unit can probably be handled without a ditto. The only problem is how to show the students the pictures of the whorls, loops, and arches. You can manage without the ditto if you think you can draw these figures satisfactorily on the blackboard or make a few copies that you can pass round and collect afterwards.

### Detective Activity

Have each student make a second complete set of prints (if this is easy to do) or a second print of one finger, probably the thumb. Divide the class into groups of approximately three students each. Have two groups exchange complete sets of prints of all members of each group, plus the extra print or prints of one member of the group. How good are the students as detectives? Can the members of each group identify to whom the "unknown" print belongs by comparing the unknown print with all the prints of the other group? Can the detectives correctly identify the owner of the print? Repeat this procedure as much as interest indicates.

### Extending the Activity

If the class seems extremely interested, you might spend some time on the classification formula for fingerprints. We admit that the system is complicated, but if you have the interest to dig it out, we think you will be able to explain it to a class. Give it a try if it appeals to you!

Why do we classify fingerprints? They are classified to provide a method of filing so sets of fingerprints can be located quickly and easily.

Pattern classification is a three-way process. It classifies prints by general shapes or contours, by the finger positions of the pattern types, and by relative size determined by ridge counts in loops and whorls.

This information is incorporated in a concise formula known as an individual's fingerprint classification. Here is a classification formula matrix that has not yet been filled in.

| Key | Major | Primary | Secondary | Subsecondary | Final |
|-----|-------|---------|-----------|--------------|-------|
|     |       |         |           |              |       |
|     |       |         |           |              |       |

Here's how it looks with some numbers in it. (This is how one person's print has actually been classified.)

| Key | Major | Primary | Secondary | Subsecondary | Final |
|-----|-------|---------|-----------|--------------|-------|
| 20  | M     | 2       | U         | 000          | 20    |
|     | L     | 4       | W         | 000          |       |

For reference, let us name each cell in the following way (N stands for numerator; D for denominator):

| 1N | 2N | 3N | 4N | 5N | 6N |
|----|----|----|----|----|----|
| 1D | 2D | 3D | 4D | 5D | 6D |

The fingerprints themselves are recorded and numbered as shown on the ditto. First let us see how the numbers are obtained for the column marked primary, that is 3N and 3D. Numerical values are arbitrarily assigned to each of the ten finger blocks as follows (The numbers are the same as those that appear on the fingerprint chart on the ditto.):

| Finger | Numerical Value | Value counts towards |
|--------|-----------------|----------------------|
| 1 (right thumb | 16 | D   Numerator or |
| 2 (right index) | 16 | N   Denominator |
| 3 | 8 | D |
| 4 | 8 | N |
| 5 | 4 | D |
| 6 | 4 | N |
| 7 | 2 | D |
| 8 | 2 | N |
| 9 | 1 | D |
| 10 (left little) | 1 | N |

The *primary* is the summation of the values assigned to those fingers whose patterns are whorls; the numerator of the primary is the summation (plus an arbitrary 1) of values of fingers 2, 4, 6, 8, 10, which are whorls, and the denominator is the summation (plus that same arbitrary 1) of values of fingers 1, 3, 5, 7, 9, whose prints are whorls. For example, if fingers 8 and 10 are whorls, the numerator will be $(2 + 1) + 1 = 4$. If fingers 7, 9, and 10 are whorls, the denominator will be $(2 + 1 + 1) + 1 = 5$. The primary for this classification will therefore be $4/5$.

Here are some practice problems:

| 1 | 2 | 3 | 4 | 5 W |
|---|---|---|---|---|
| 6 | 7 | 8 | 9 W | 10 W |

In this example, finger 10 is the only finger that counts toward the numerator which has a whorl. Therefore, $N = (1) + 1 = 2$. Fingers 5 and 9 are fingers that have whorls *(W)* and that count for the denominator. Therefore, $D = (4 + 1) + 1 = 6$. The primary for this example is $2/6$.

| 1 | 2 | 3 | 4 | 5 |
|---|---|---|---|---|
| 6 | 7 W | 8 W | 9 W | 10 W |

$N = (2 + 1) + 1 = 4$
$D = (2 + 1) + 1 = 4$
**Primary is 4/4**

| 1 | 2 | 3 | 4 | 5 |
|---|---|---|---|---|
| 6 W | 7 W | 8 | 9 W | 10 W |

$N = (4 + 1) + 1 = 6$
$D = (2 + 1) + 1 = 4$
**Primary is 6/4**

| 1 | 2 | 3 | 4 | 5 |
|---|---|---|---|---|
| 6 W | 7 W | 8 W | 9 W | 10 W |

$N = (4 + 2 + 1) + 1 = 8$
$D = (2 + 1) + 1 = 4$
**Primary is 8/4**

| 1 | 2 | 3 | 4 | 5 |
|---|---|---|---|---|
| 6 | 7 | 8 W | 9 W | 10 W |

$N = (2 + 1) + 1 = 4$
$D = (8) + 1 = 9$
**Primary is 4/9**

The **key** (1N) is obtained by counting, beginning with the right thumb, the ridges of the first loop appearing on the fingerprint card. The little fingers are excluded since they are reserved for the **final**. The **major** (2N and 2D) is derived from the thumbs. When whorls appear, it reflects the whorl tracings. When loops appear, the ridge counts as *S, M, L* (small, medium, or large.) The numerator gives the information for the right thumb; the denominator gives the information for the left thumb. The **secondary** (4N and 4D) records, in capital letters, the type of pattern appearing in the index fingers of each hand. Again, the numerator is the right index finger, the denominator the left index finger. In the **subsecondary** (5N and 5D), the numerator looks at second, third, fourth fingers; the denominator looks at seventh, eighth, ninth fingers. Here, ridge counts of loops and ridge tracings of whorls are given letters which describe certain characteristics. The **final** (6N only) is one number. This is the ridge count of the loop in the right little finger. If that finger is not a loop, the ridge count of the left little finger is used instead.

# HIDDEN ELEMENTS

A chemical element is a substance that cannot be broken further into more elementary substances by ordinary chemical means.

Twenty-nine elements are hidden here!! Find them hidden horizontally, vertically, or diagonally.

|    | 1 | 2 | 3 | 4 | 5 | 6 | 7 | 8 | 9 | 10 | 11 | 12 | 13 |
|----|---|---|---|---|---|---|---|---|---|----|----|----|----|
| P  | I | N | D | I | U | M | A | N | B | H  | C  | D  | E  |
| O  | Z | I | N | C | F | E | O | X | E | N  | O  | N  | G  |
| N  | K | T | H | D | I | R | J | L | K | O  | O  | M  | R  |
| M  | L | R | L | M | O | C | I | N | O | R  | U  | E  | P  |
| L  | Q | O | Y | B | R | U | H | S | T | I  | P  | N  | N  |
| K  | G | G | U | P | M | R | V | L | S | P  | E  | O  | N  |
| J  | W | E | A | X | T | Y | Y | E | O | G  | B  | O  | Z  |
| I  | A | N | B | L | C | O | N | C | Y | R  | D  | D  | M  |
| H  | E | F | G | H | L | G | N | X | A | A  | I  | U  | I  |
| G  | N | O | G | R | A | I | O | C | R | J  | I  | N  | K  |
| F  | A | L | U | M | I | N | U | M | L | D  | M  | N  | E  |
| E  | P | L | A | T | I | N | U | M | O | O  | P  | Q  | R  |
| D  | E | F | G | C | H | I | J | S | I | L  | V  | E  | R  |
| C  | K | L | K | M | O | L | Y | B | D | E  | N  | U  | M  |
| B  | M | E | N | O | P | M | U | I | D | A  | N  | A  | V  |
| A  | L | S | I | L | I | C | O | N | F | D  | L  | O  | G  |

## Using Hidden Elements

Each student may work individually to discover as many hidden elements as he can. You may list the hidden elements on the board or on a transparency for projection on an overhead projector.

Instead of having students work alone, you may have the class participate in the group game described below.

**Object:** To discover the largest number of hidden elements.

**Student groupings:** By teams.

**The Play:** Members of teams take turns giving the location of elements they have discovered. Note the columns and rows of the ditto have been marked for easy reference.

**Scoring:** Give two points for each discovery *before* you post the list of hidden elements. Give one point for each discovery *after* you post the list of hidden elements. (For material on how to keep a running score, see Hint 5, Hints for Using the Materials, the Introduction.)

**Note:** You, the teacher, post the list after the students have exhausted the elements they can discover without it.

### Special five-point questions:

1. Two hidden elements appear twice. Name one of these. *Answer:* gold, lead

2. Diamond and graphite are different forms of which element? *Answer:* carbon

3. Which two elements are the principle constituents of glass? *Answer:* silicon

4. Which is the most common element in the Earth's crust? *Answer:* silicon (major); aluminum, iron, magnesium; sodium; small amounts of copper, gold, silver, lead, zinc, and tin.

5. Name an element that is a gas. *Answer:* argon, chlorine, nitrogen, oxygen, helium, krypton, neon, radon, xenon.

6. Name an element that is an inert gas. (There are several). *Answer:* argon, helium, krypton, neon, radon, xenon

7. Which element of those listed is the lightest metal (has the least density)? *Answer:* magnesium

8. Which element of those listed is the heaviest metal (has the greatest density)? *Answer:* platinum (greatest); iron (next greatest)

9. Which element is the foundation stone of organic chemistry—that is, it is basic to life. *Answer:* carbon

## Answers to *Hidden Elements*

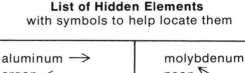

| **List of Hidden Elements** with symbols to help locate them | |
|---|---|
| aluminum → | molybdenum → |
| argon ← | neon ↖ |
| boron ↗ | nickel ↙ |
| carbon ↗ | nitrogen ↓ |
| chlorine ↘ | oxygen ↗ |
| copper ↗ | platinum → |
| gallium ↘ | radon ↗ |
| gold ↗ ← | silicon → |
| helium ↙ | silver → |
| indium → | sodium ↗ |
| iron ↑ | tin ↑ |
| krypton ↘ | vanadium ← |
| lead ↓ | xenon → |
| magnesium ↗ | zinc → |
| mercury ↓ | |

## Solution:

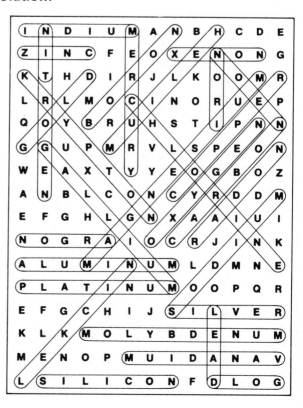

# INVENTION or DISCOVERY

In Column A, match the inventors (discoverers) with their inventions (discoveries).

In Column B, if the item is an invention, mark I; if a discovery, mark D.

| A | B | Inventions and Discoveries | Inventors and Discoverers |
|---|---|---|---|
| | | 1. adding machine | a. Banting, Sir Frederick |
| | | 2. airplane | b. Beebe, Charles |
| | | 3. aqualung | c. Bell, Alexander G. |
| | | 4. bathysphere | d. Birdseye, Clarence |
| | | 5. cotton gin | e. Bunsen, Robert W. |
| | | 6. cyclotron | f. Burroughs, William |
| | | 7. deuterium | g. Colt, Samuel |
| | | 8. diesel engine | h. Cousteau, Jacques Ives |
| | | 9. dynamite | i. Daguerre, Louis |
| | | 10. electric battery | j. Diesel, Rudolf |
| | | 11. electric motor | k. Eastman, George |
| | | 12. elevator | l. Edison, Thomas A. |
| | | 13. gas burner | m. Einstein, Albert |
| | | 14. gyroscopic compass | n. Fahrenheit, Gabriel D. |
| | | 15. helicopter | o. Faraday, Michael |
| | | 16. incandescent filament lamp | p. Fleming, Sir Alexander |
| | | 17. insulin | q. Franklin, Benjamin |
| | | 18. Kodak camera | r. Goodyear, Charles |
| | | 19. lightning rod | s. Jenner, Edward |
| | | 20. lock (pin tumbler cylinder) | t. Joliot-Curie, Irène and Frédéric |
| | | 21. mercurial thermometer | u. Judson, Whitcomb L. |
| | | 22. motion picture machine | v. Land, Edwin H. |
| | | 23. oxygen | w. Lavoisier, Antoine L. |
| | | 24. penicillin | x. Lawrence, Ernest O. |
| | | 25. phonograph | y. Marconi, Marchese G. |
| | | 26. photoelectric effect | z. McCormick, Cyrus Hall |
| | | 27. photography | aa. Morse, Samuel F. B. |
| | | 28. Polaroid Land camera | bb. Nobel, Alfred B. |
| | | 29. quick freezing of food | cc. Otis, Elisha Graves |
| | | 30. radioactive isotopes | dd. Priestly, Joseph |
| | | 31. reaper | ee. Roentgen, Wilhelm K. |
| | | 32. revolver | ff. Sikorsky, Igor |
| | | 33. smallpox vaccination | gg. Sperry, Elmer A. |
| | | 34. telegraph | hh. Urey, Harold C. |
| | | 35. telephone | ii. Volta, Alessandro |
| | | 36. television | jj. Whitney, Eli |
| | | 37. vulcanized rubber | kk. Wright, Wilbur and Orville |
| | | 38. wireless telegraph | ll. Yale, Linus, Jr. |
| | | 39. X-ray | mm. Zworykin, Vladimir K. |
| | | 40. zipper | |

## Answers to *Invention or Discovery*

| Invention/ Discovery | Inventor/ Discoverer | Invention or Discovery | Date | Nationality of *I* or *D* |
|---|---|---|---|---|
| 1 | f | I | 1888 | American |
| 2 | kk | I | 1903 | American |
| 3 | h | I | 1943 | French |
| 4 | b | I | 1930 | American |
| 5 | jj | I | 1793 | American |
| 6 | x | I | 1931 | American |
| 7 | hh | D | 1932 | American |
| 8 | j | I | 1898 | German |
| 9 | bb | I | 1866 | Swedish |
| 10 | ii | I | 1800 | Italian |
| 11 | o | I | 1821 | British |
| 12 | cc | I | 1852 | American |
| 13 | e | I | 1855 | German |
| 14 | gg | I | 1910 | American |
| 15 | ff | I | 1939 | American |
| 16 | l | I | 1879 | American |
| 17 | a | D | 1922 | Canadian |
| 18 | k | I | 1888 | American |
| 19 | q | I | 1752 | American |
| 20 | ll | I | 1865 | American |
| 21 | n | I | 1714 | German |
| 22 | l | I | 1893 | American |
| 23 | dd and w | D | 1775ish | British and French |
| 24 | p | D | 1928 | British |
| 25 | l | I | 1877 | American |
| 26 | m | D | 1905 | German |
| 27 | i | I | 1839 | French |
| 28 | v | I | 1947 | American |
| 29 | d | I | 1924 | American |
| 30 | t | D | 1933 | French |
| 31 | z | I | 1831 | American |
| 32 | g | I | 1835 | American |
| 33 | s | D | 1796 | British |
| 34 | aa | I | 1837 | American |
| 35 | c | I | 1876 | American |
| 36 | mm | I | 1923 | American |
| 37 | r | D | 1839 | American |
| 38 | y | I | 1896 | Italian |
| 39 | ee | D | 1895 | German |
| 40 | u | I | 1893 | American |

## Using Invention or Discovery

Permit students to use encyclopedias or other research books if they are available. Students may work individually categorizing their data. Do this as long as the class seems absorbed. When interest lags, have students pool their knowledge to complete their data. Then you might want to play the following game or explore the discussion questions.

## Invention or Discovery Game

**Object:** To win points for matching in one or more categories.

**Materials:** Each student has copy of the ditto page, or access to that information (transparency, blackboard).

**Student groupings:** Teams.

**The play:** Possible categories for play—

1. Match discovery or invention to discoverer or inventor. Team A calls out item from first column; then calls match from second column. Or Team A calls out item from first column; Team B replies with item from second column. Whichever method of play is adopted, that method should be followed for the entire period.

2. Match discoverer or inventor to nationality.

3. Is item in Column A a discovery, or is it an invention?

4. What is the century in which the discovery or invention was made?

**Scoring:** One point for each correct answer.

**Note:** Students should keep a record of correct answers. These will be useful for the discussion questions because some of those questions are based on the completed data.

**Discussion Questions:** These are difficult questions. Encourage students to explore them fully.

1. What is the difference between an invention and a discovery? How would you classify streptomycin? *Answer: discovery.* How would you classify dynamite? *Answer: invention.* How would you classify vulcanized rubber? *Answer: discovery.* (It is often hard to tell the difference between an invention and a discovery. One *invents* something that did not exist before. One *discovers* something that existed before it was found. For example, Galileo discovered sunspots, because they always existed.

But Edison invented the phonograph because it did not exist before he made it. Invention involves an act of creation. However, discovery may also involve an act of creation. For example, Fleming discovered penicillin because penicillin is a mold that exists in nature. It had been previously known that mold existed that would destroy bacteria. However, Fleming created the idea that this substance (penicillin) could be extracted from mold. It was this idea that led to the discovery of penicillin. How do people decide who invented or discovered something? One discovery in the list is assigned to two men. Who are they, and what is the discovery? What do you make of this?

2. Do you notice any countries surprisingly absent from this list? Do you notice a preponderance of inventions and discoveries from one particular country? Which country? What do you make of all this? Much of this data was taken from an American encyclopedia. Does this have any bearing on the people credited with making inventions or discoveries? (See the last part of question 1.)

3. One inventor has three inventions ascribed to him. Who is he? Are any other people on our list known to be very inventive? Is it surprising that one person should have made many inventions? What do you think?

4. Dates of discoveries and inventions sometimes vary from source to source. It is sometimes difficult to assign a specific date to a discovery or invention. Why do you think this is so?

5. Which of these inventors were probably involved in the marketing of their inventions, because they have products or companies named after them? *Answers:* Burroughs adding machine; Bell Telephone; Colt revolver; Edison phonograph; Otis elevator; Yale lock; Birds-eye frozen foods; Sperry gyroscope.

# NOW YOU SEE IT, Now you don't

**Object:** To find blind spots in the eyes.

**Student groupings:** By pairs.

**Materials:** A 3 by 5 index card for each pupil, or cut or tear a piece of paper of approximately that size.

**Preparation:** Each student should mark his card as shown:

You may draw this card on the blackboard for the students to copy, or you may make an example and hold it up for the class to see.

**Procedure:** With his left eye covered, the student holds the card at arm's length in front of him and looks at the cross with his right eye. He moves the card slowly toward him until he can no longer see the spot. This is the blind spot for his right eye.

The student turns the card around so the dot is to the left of the cross. He closes his right eye and repeats the experiment to locate the blind spot for his left eye.

While one student finds his own blind spot, the second student in the pair can record the distance of the card from the cheek or brow of the experimenter. If rulers are available, they are excellent to use. If they are not, the class, or you, may decide on a unit of measure, such as the length of a sheet of paper.

**Conclusion:** The entire back of the eye (the retina) is light sensitive in all but one place—where the main eye nerve from the brain joins the eye.

**Recording of data:** Distance of blindspot from left eye. Distance of blindspot from right eye. Are these distances the same? Are they different?

**Coordinating of data:** On the blackboard (each student might keep this record too). Tabulate distances from left eye for each student. Tabulate distances from right eye for each student. What is the class average distance for the left eye? What is the class average distance for the right eye? You might wish to look at the data for boys versus girls. Is there any significant difference? How about students who wear glasses versus those who do not? Any difference?

## Another Experiment

**Materials:** Two pencils.

**Procedure:** The student holds two pencils apart, at about arm's length, tips pointing toward each other. He closes one eye and tries to bring the two pencil points together.

**Conclusion:** Eliminating one eye makes it impossible to see two dimensionally. This ability is needed to join objects that may be approaching along different planes.

**Variation:** Try this experiment with the student using one finger of each hand instead of two pencils. Why is this easier?

### An Enrichment for the Teacher

Several of the units in this science section consist of explorations which involve collecting data and organizing this data into some kind of matrix for easy analysis. In some of the experiments we have asked you to look at the data for boys vs. girls . . . a classification which is readily at hand in co-ed schools. Note that this is merely one of many possible ways to sort this data. Encourage your class to explore other, possibly more fruitful methods of classifying data than our arbitrary suggestions for the different experiments. Here are some examples of the kinds of things we have in mind.

In the hands crossing experiment for example, we would guess that the classification of boys vs. girls would yield roughly the same results for each. However, try looking at the data for right-handed vs. left-handed people. It may be different now.

In the pulse rates . . . compare rates of individuals when standing or sitting with rates after they have jumped in position twenty times. Here it might be useful to look at athletes vs. non-athletes. (Admittedly, you might have to get class agreement on how to determine who is an athlete . . . perhaps one who is a member of a school athletic team.) Here you might collect your data as follows:

|  | Average pulse rate: no exercise | Average pulse rate: after exercise |
|---|---|---|
| non-athlete |  |  |
| athlete |  |  |

An extremely important lesson your students might learn from these experiments is that data is affected by the manner in which it is presented. The same data, presented in different ways, might lead to completely different conclusions. We have no doubt that much of what makes the gifted scientist is the ability to perceive a way of organizing data to make a clear statement or conclusion. The educated person should also learn that this may be a two edged sword, and should be critical of how material is presented before he draws conclusions from it.

# PHRENOLOGY

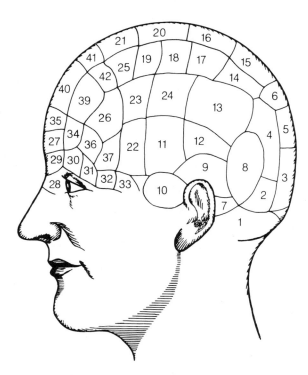

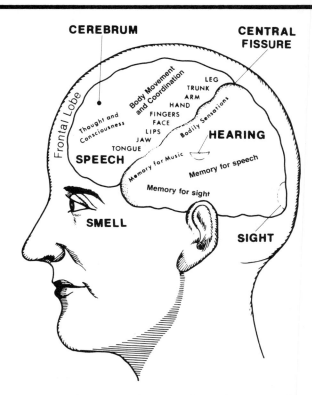

On the left is a mapping of a phrenological head. The numbers locate regions that were thought to be the seat (organ) of particular characteristics, or attributes. The chart below gives the supposed attribute, together with its original definition. The head on the right is mapped according to present theory. Notice, although centers are specifically located, they refer to specific physiological processes rather than the psychological attributes of phrenology.

1. Amativeness—love and attraction towards the opposite sex
2. Conjugal love—constancy towards matrimonial partner
3. Parental love—love of children, animals and pets
4. Friendship—desire to form friendships, sociability
5. Inhabitiveness—love of home and country
6. Continuity—concentrativeness, application, connectedness
7. Vitativeness—love of life, resistance to disease
8. Combativeness—courage, bravery, aggressiveness
9. Executiveness—force, energy, endurance, extermination
10. Alimentiveness—sense of hunger and thirst, appetite for food
11. Acquisitiveness—desire to acquire, accumulate, economize
12. Secretiveness—concealment of thoughts and emotions, reserve
13. Cautiousness—prudence in danger, carefulness, fear
14. Approbativeness—desire for popularity and approval
15. Self-esteem—dignity, self-respect, love of independence
16. Firmness—stability, perseverance, steadfastness
17. Conscientiousness—sense of right, justice, integrity
18. Hope—expectation, anticipation, perfect trust
19. Spirituality—faith, spiritual belief, love of the marvelous
20. Veneration—reverence, respect for superiority, age, antiquity
21. Benevolence—sympathy, kindness, desire to do good
22. Constructiveness—ingenuity, invention, mechanical ability
23. Ideality—taste, love of beauty, poetry and art, imagination
24. Sublimity—perception of the vast, sublime, infinite
25. Imitation—ability to imitate; aptitude, versatility
26. Mirth—perception of wit, fun, facetiousness, ridicule
27. Individuality—aptitude for observation, perceptive power
28. Form—perception and memory of faces, forms, resemblances
29. Size—ability to judge proportions, bulk, size, distance, and so on
30. Weight—control of motion, balancing, equilibrium
31. Color—power of distinguishing and harmonizing colors, shades, and so on
32. Order—neatness, method, arrangement, desire to work by rules
33. Calculation—talent for calculating and remembering figures
34. Locality—recognition and remembrance of localities, positions, places
35. Eventuality—memory of passing events, facts, news, and so on
36. Time—appreciation and recollection of time, periods, seasons
37. Tune—love of music, appreciation of harmony, sound, and so on
38. Language—ability to talk, learn languages, remember words
39. Causality—originality of thought, ability to plan, reason, and so on
40. Comparison—ability to illustrate, classify, criticize, compare
41. Human Nature—intuition; discernment of character and motives
42. Suavity—agreeableness, affability, persuasiveness, desire to please

English
Social Studies Science
Class
Individuals
Dittos

Phrenology was the name given to a system of psychology based on experience and observation rather than scientific research. It was developed by F. J. Gall about 1800. Phrenologists believed that each mental faculty was located in a definite region of the surface of the brain. The size of this region supposedly caused corresponding changes in the shape of the skull. Therefore, by examining the shape of the skull for bumps and so forth the phrenologist could assess the abilities and personality of the subject. Although the theory became very popular for a time, by the early 1900s, it had been largely discredited by scientific research. It was in its attempt to localize certain specific functions of the brain (memory and intelligence, for example) that phrenology went wrong! Modern science believes that these kinds of characteristics depend on the total composition of the brain and cannot be localized in any specific part of it.

Complete the puzzle, using vocabulary from the phrenological chart. Definitions and numbers of letters for each word are given below.

### Definition

| | |
|---|---|
| **4**–letter words | Love of music |
| | Memory of faces |
| | Recollection of periods |
| | Expectation, trust |
| | Ability to judge distance |
| **5**–letter words | Neatness, method |
| | Fun, wit |
| **6**–letter words | Control of motion |
| **7**–letter words | agreeableness |
| **8**–letter words | ability to talk |
| | taste, love of beauty |
| **9**–letter words | aptitude, versatility |
| | perception of vast, infinite |

| | |
|---|---|
| **10**-letter words | application |
| | ability to illustrate, classify |
| | sociability |
| | PHRENOLOGY |
| | dignity |
| | reverence |
| **11**-letter words | talent for figures |
| | attraction towards the opposite sex |
| **12**-letter words | love of life |
| | constancy |
| **13**-letter words | aptitude for observation |
| | concealment, reserve |
| **15**-letter words | desire for approval |
| **16**-letter words | ingenuity, mechanical ability |

120

## Answers to *Phrenology*

4-letter words: tune
form
time
hope
size
5-letter words: order
mirth
6-letter words: weight
7-letter words: suavity
8-letter words: language
ideality
9-letter words: imitation
sublimity
10-letter words: continuity
comparison
friendship
PHRENOLOGY
self-esteem
veneration
11-letter words: calculation
amativeness
12-letter words: vitativeness
conjugal love
13-letter words: individuality
secretiveness

15-letter words: approbativeness
16-letter words: constructiveness

## An Exercise in Phrenology

It's amusing to read how a prominent phrenologist picked the particular region of the brain to which he ascribed the location of a particular organ and faculty. These regions were initially determined by studying common characteristics of skulls of people having strong tendencies toward these attributes. Below are the descriptions of some attributes. Have students guess which attribute the phrenologist was referring to. (Students may refer to their list of attributes.)

1. This part of the skull is more prominent in apes and women than in men. *Answer:* parental love

2. This bulge was noticed on head of a musical prodigy of five. *Answer:* tune

3. When Gall, the developer of phrenology, visited churches, he noticed that those who prayed with the most fervor were prominent in this region. This region was also prominent in a pious brother. *Answer:* veneration

4. This rising was noticed on the head of the highly regarded servant of a friend, as well as on a kindly

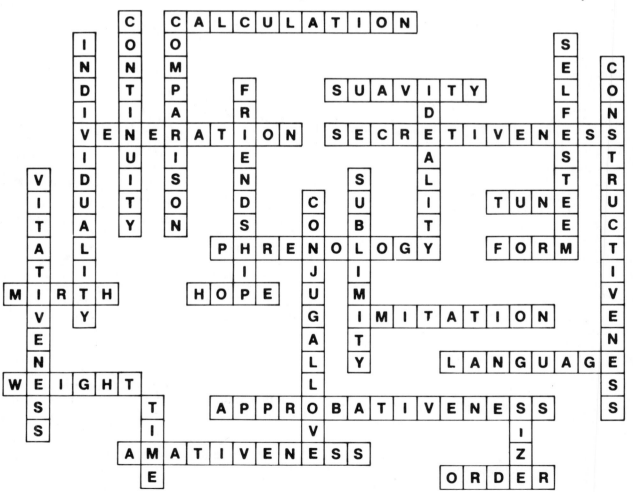

schoolmate who nursed his brothers and sisters when they were ill. *Answer:* benevolence

5. This organ gives a wide interval between the eyes. It was found in a squinting girl with a good memory for faces. *Answer:* form

6. This was the first organ noticed by Gall. His clever school fellow, quick at languages, had prominent eyes. Old authors have noted the connection between prominent eyeballs and mental development. *Answer:* language

7. This organ was described as being large in a gourmand acquaintance, and was therefore supposed to be the organ of selecting food. *Answer:* alimentiveness

8. This was the region in which Gall saw a protuberance on the head of a lunatic who fancied herself the queen of France. *Answer:* approbativeness

9. This was placed in a region where a churchman of hesitating disposition and a vacillating statesman both had large protrusions. *Answer:* cautiousness

10. This organ was located on top of the head because it had been pointed out that people of determination had lofty heads. *Answer:* firmness

11. This region was very prominent at the top of the bare region of the forehead of a wise friend of Gall's. This friend was fond of analogies. *Answer:* comparison

12. This region, on each side of *comparison,* was noticed to be very prominent on a bust of the famous philosopher Kant. It was considered the seat of the faculty correlating cause and effect. *Answer:* causality

## Practical Uses of Phrenology

Today, people give written tests to determine aptitudes.

In the past, people could consult the phrenologist about aptitude. Have students look at the list of attributes and guess when a phrenologist might be helpful.

1. Choosing a profession: Parents sought consultations with phrenologists to help them decide for which professions and jobs to prepare their children. Businessmen consulted phrenologists to decide how to place prospective employees.

2. Choosing a marriage partner: Suitable matrimonial partners supposedly had attributes that would harmonize rather than antagonize. What are some combinations that might cause trouble? (Both partners firm and inconsistent. Both partners avaricious, greedy for wealth. Both partners unsympathetic. Both partners weak in moral qualities.)

3. Classifying: Ask whether particular attributes seem grouped around a particular area by phrenologists? For example, the top of the head—lofty or moral attributes (veneration, spirituality, hope, benevolence, conscientiousness) the back of the head—domestic attributes; front of the head—intellectuality; the rest—animal propensities, qualities that provide for man's animal wants and assist him in self-preservation and self-protection.

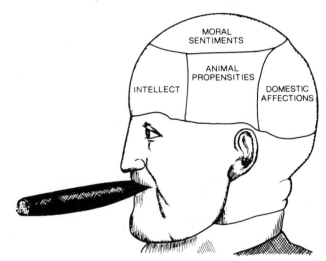

## Phrenological Mapping Compared With Modern Mapping (See diagram on p. 119.)

Both the modern mapping and the phrenological mapping seem to place the highest functions of the brain in the prefrontal area. This area is now thought to be the highest center of the brain, the seat of thinking and cerebrating. The phrenologists assigned the attributes of so-called intellectuality (memory, analysis, etc.) to this area. This is the region that is more highly developed in man than in animals. (For example, this region is very small in dogs.) Memory for music and tune seems to be in the same area.

There's a large discrepancy between phrenological and modern mapping at the top of the head. To this area phrenologists assigned the so-called moral sentiments. Modern scientists believe that the controls for motor areas are here. Alimentiveness, or the appetite for food, seems to be located in the same place in both analyses, although modern science sees the appetite for food as a complicated series of chemical and mechanical interrelationships controlled by the hypothalamus.

# PHYSICS FUN

Here are a few experiments that your students may find amusing. While they're enjoying themselves, you will be demonstrating some fundamental ideas of physics—friction and Bernoûilli's principle.

## Friction

**Materials:** A yardstick or ruler.

**Procedure:** Balance a ruler or yardstick on two extended index fingers, letting one end of the ruler extend much further than the other end. Ask the students to guess which way the stick will fall if you move your fingers toward each other. Record the results of the guess. (You will probably find that most students will guess the stick will fall toward the protruding end.) Have the students take turns coming to the front of the room to try the experiment. This should be rather amusing.

What actually happens is that the stick falls neither way. It always balances in the center. As you try to move your fingers together, only one finger will move until both fingers are equidistant from the center. At that point, both fingers will move to meet at the center.

**Analysis:** What prevents the other finger from moving? The answer is friction. The amount that each finger can slide is a function of the proportion of the weight of the stick that bears down on it. Because the finger toward the center bears the greater amount of this weight, it cannot slide until the other finger is equally near the center.

## Bernoûilli's Principle

These next two experiments both demonstrate Bernoûilli's principle. You should be easily able to locate the equipment you will need to try them. Both of these experiments will yield unexpected results. Encourage as many students as are willing to come up and try them. Everyone will enjoy watching the attempts. Allow as much time as students want to try their turn. Then share each other's conjectures. Ask who can describe what seems to be happening. Ask why they think it is so. Have them describe orally or write why they think it is so. Have students try to make a diagram.

## Paper Blow Experiment I

**Materials:** An empty cold drink can or bottle. A piece of paper or tissue approximately ½ inch by 1½ inch. (This should be small enough to drop in the bottle easily)

**Procedure:** Place the piece of paper on the rim of the opening, in position to be blown in. Try to drop the paper into the container by blowing on it. Ask volunteers to come to the front of the class to try to blow the paper in.

## Paper Blow Experiment II

**Material:** Two books of approximately the same size. A sheet of paper.

**Procedure:** Place the two books on a surface about three or four inches apart. Place the sheet of paper over and between them.

Try to lift the paper by blowing horizontally underneath it.

## Analysis of Experiments I and II

The effect you are seeing here is Bernoûilli's effect. (Daniel Bernoûilli was a Swiss physicist who lived and worked in the first half of the eighteenth century.)

When the velocity of a fluid is increased, (and air may be regarded as such a fluid), the pressure *inside* that fluid is decreased. This creates the force that makes it possible for airplanes to fly. The air streaming over the top of an airplane wing gives it most of its lift. The upward curve of the top of the wing surface forces the air to travel more swiftly (with greater velocity) over the top of the wing. This creates a reduced air pressure on top. Because of this, the pressure below the wing is greater than the pressure above, and this greater pressure underneath creates the lift that keeps the plane flying.

In the bottle and tissue experiment, the attempt to blow the tissue into the bottle increases the velocity and therefore, decreases the pressure of the air outside the bottle. The pressure of the air inside the bottle is now greater than the pressure outside. This causes the tissue to fly out and away, rather than into, the bottle.

The same principle is at work when one blows under the paper across the books. The greater velocity beneath causes a decreased air pressure beneath. Therefore, the pressure of the air above is now greater, and the paper is pressed down. If you blow horizontally across the top of the paper, the opposite will happen, and the paper will flutter up.

# SPACE: Games, Puzzles, Simulations

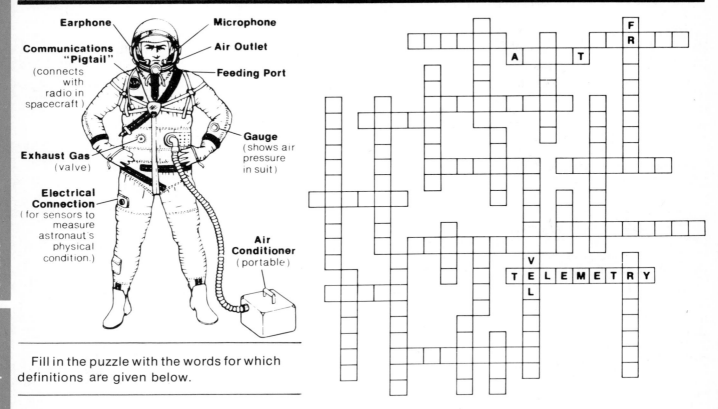

Earphone

Communications "Pigtail"
(connects with radio in spacecraft.)

Exhaust Gas
(valve)

Electrical Connection
(for sensors to measure astronaut's physical condition.)

Microphone

Air Outlet

Feeding Port

Gauge
(shows air pressure in suit)

Air Conditioner
(portable)

Fill in the puzzle with the words for which definitions are given below.

---

4-letter words:
  planet; god of war
  National Aeronautics and Space Administration (abv.)
  pause in countdown to clear up difficulty

5-letter words:
  to halt a spaceflight
  path of satellite around parent body
  planet; goddess of beauty
  propulsion unit of rocket
  unmanned spacecraft put into outer space
  planet that is most remote in solar system; approximate size of moon

6-letter words:
  planet; name is heavy metallic element
  propelling force provided by rocket engines
  self-contained unit of spacecraft

7-letter words:
  container on rocket, for men, animals, or instruments, to be recovered after flight
  spacecraft's descent into earth's atmosphere
  planet; smallest one
  planet; largest one
  rocket engine used to set vehicle in motion

8-letter words:
  order to destroy misfunctioning rocket after leaving launch pad
  to follow path of space vehicle by instrument

9-letter words:
  body that revolves about larger body
  platform from which rocket is launched
  *telemetry:* obtaining a measurement from one place (satellite, for example) and transmitting it to another place such as a tracking station on earth
  U.S. title for its space pilots.
  "Sailor of the Universe"; U.S.S.R. name for its space pilots.

10-letter words:
  spacecraft covering; absorbs heat, protects during reentry
  material burned in rocket to provide thrust
  in-flight meeting of spacecrafts
  unpowered flight while in orbit

11-letter word:
  rocket; slows down space vehicle; fires opposite direction to main rocket

14-letter word:
  speed when object escapes gravitational pull of body launching it

## Additional Puzzles

Draw this array on the board, filling in only the word "spacesuit." Have students fill in spaces vertically, using parts of space suit shown on ditto page.

Here's a puzzle for you to put on the board. It uses the names of the planets. Remember, as in the spacesuit puzzle above, draw the puzzle to include all the squares that are to be filled in. However, fill in only the word *planet* in its appropriate line of squares. Here also, the planets are filled in vertically.

### Answers to Telemetry Puzzle on the Student Page

4—letter words: Mars  NASA  hold
5—letter words: abort  orbit  Venus  probe  stage  Pluto
6—letter words: Uranus  thrust  module
7—letter words: capsule  reentry  Mercury  Jupiter  booster
8—letter words: destruct  tracking
9—letter words: satellite  launch pad  telemetry  astronaut  cosmonaut
10—letter words: heatshield  propellant  rendezvous  freeflight
11—letter word: retrorocket
14—letter word: escape velocity

Here are some activities that will apply to a broad spectrum of ability levels. If students have difficulty getting started, give them some hints. In the Telemetry puzzle, for example, fill in additional terms from the answer sheet if necessary. The Simulation Game can be great fun, but it should be used only for classes that present no discipline problems or that you know from prior substitute experience. There is a great deal more than one period's material in these activities. Don't try to pack them into a single class meeting!

## Simulation Game

Among the projected space plans for the future are space station laboratories. Ask students what kinds of scientists would be interested in a science laboratory satellite. What experiments could be done in the space laboratory that scientists would be unable to do as easily, or at all, on earth?

Begin a simulation game. A simulation game is one in which students assume roles in a given real life situation. They learn from acting out these roles. You may use the information below as a guide to help the students define their roles.

**Setting:** A congressional hearing of the National Committee for Space Exploration.

**Subject:** The Federal space budget for next year, with special focus on design and development of an orbiting space laboratory.

**Actors:** Lobbyists interested in doing experiments in such a laboratory; Members of the committee. (Each student has two roles. He acts as a committee member when he is not performing as a lobbyist.)

**The game:** Establish, with the class, the different kinds of scientist that might be interested in the space lab. (See the following information on scientists so you can use it when you need to feed in ideas.) To save time, you might list the scientists on the board.

Divide the class into groups of three to five students each. Each group will act as lobbyists for one of the scientific professions discussed. Give groups about five to ten minutes to discuss together why they want to be included in the plans for the space laboratory. How do they justify the need for their piece of the pie? (Again, use the following information to help groups get started.) Each group will present its case to the committee.

Remember that the important question to justify (and perhaps you might clue the committee to ask it) is: What experiments could be done in the space laboratory which you, as scientists, would be unable to do as easily, if at all, on earth? The lobbyists should suggest what the group they represent intends to study, and why these studies are important.

Convene the hearing. Permit each group to present its appeal. Then the committee (the class) meets to formulate a report and make recommendations. The committee may vote on which groups have worthwhile plans. It may vote to establish orders of priority. It may vote on how to distribute funds among the different groups of scientists.

## Information on Scientists

**Astronomer:** The astronomer would be able to make his observations free from the effects of the veil of haze of the earth's atmosphere. His telescopes in the station would reveal more about the universe than do his telescopes on Earth. For example, by studying the behavior of stars and attempting to learn how they are formed by the interstellar dust and gases, he might obtain clues to the birth of the universe and what it might do in the future. This would be accomplished by the observation of ultraviolet light which Earth telescopes cannot observe since this light is absorbed in the Earth's atmosphere.

**Physicist:** The physicist might seek powerful new energy sources for use on Earth in mysterious deep space x-rays, which stream from sources such as pulsars, quasars, and radio galaxies. The physicist could perform experiments to check the laws of nature and test scientific theories. For example, by comparing time kept by atomic clocks in the space station to clocks on Earth, he could test Einstein's theory of relativity. The physicist could study various types of radiation—cosmic rays, x-rays, and the Van Allen belt (the trapped radiation around the earth created by the interaction of the earth's magnetic field and the charge on particles). The physicist might also want to investigate the structure of the outer atmosphere, its composition, its degree of ionization, the effects of solar radiation, and the effect of space environment on materials and processes. He might also be interested in the physics of meteoric particle erosion processes.

**Biologist:** The biologist would try to learn more about the growth of plants and animals in an environment free from Earth's gravitational force, its regular changes of night and day, and the attractions of the moon. The biologist would study the effects of space radiation on living cells. He might pursue the search for extraterritorial life and independent evolutionary systems, which constitute the new science known as exobiology.

**Botanist:** The botanist would study plants growing in an environment free from Earth's biological rhythms—one in which light is different and the gravitational fields are weaker than is that of Earth.

**Medical doctor:** The doctor might be interested in experiments in which they could observe the effect of weightlessness on the human body.

**Meteorologist:** The meteorologist would study the stars, sun, solar wind, and the Earth's upper atmosphere and magnetic field.

**Geologist:** The geologist might be interested in the capture and chemical analysis or recovery of meteoric particles to compare with data from meteorites.

**Psychologist:** The psychologist might study man's psychological reaction to weightlessness, isolation, disorientation, and so on.

Perhaps you can think of other scientists who might be interested in using the space laboratory.

## For discussion

There are many different kinds of satellites, serving many different functions. See how much of the following information can be drawn from your class.

What kinds of satellites are there? What do they do? How are they useful?

**Communications satellites:** Provide TV channels for television transmission between continents. Provide an inexpensive communications relay system. Provide radio communication of wide range of frequency.

**Meteorological satellites:** Provide improved weather forecasts, by obtaining pictures of earth's cloud cover. Provide early warning of impending hurricanes and tornadoes. Keep track of solar energy loss by measuring heat radiated from the earth.

**Navigational satellites:** Provide accurate fix on positions of ships in all kinds of weather, therefore preventing collisions between ships.

**Geodetic satellites:** Use trigonometry to check the size and shape of the Earth. Help to achieve accurate mapmaking (cartography).

**Military satellites:** There are many kinds of these. Communication satellites provide fast, reliable communication which is always necessary to the military. Navigation satellites provide accurate fix on ship positions and aid in detection of nuclear tests in space. Surveillance satellites provide detection.

**Earth resource satellites:** (These are very new.) Provide continued study of various earth resources such as water, timber, crops, minerals, and land use. Detect large-scale effects of surface processes such as water erosion.

**Satellites without instruments:** Even without instruments, satellites can give new information about the size and shape of the earth from changes in the orbits they follow. Such observations have led to the conclusion that Earth is more nearly spherical than had been thought.

**Scientific satellites:** See Simulation Game

# The World is a Freshwater Pond
## An Exploration in Ecology

F O O D C H A I N

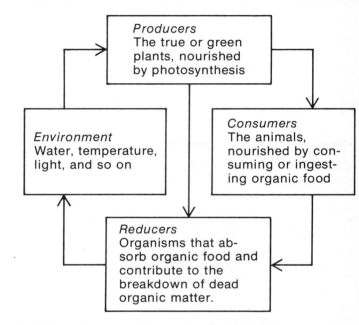

**Producers**
The true or green plants, nourished by photosynthesis

**Environment**
Water, temperature, light, and so on

**Consumers**
The animals, nourished by consuming or ingesting organic food

**Reducers**
Organisms that absorb organic food and contribute to the breakdown of dead organic matter.

Can you complete the puzzle, using items from the pond community below? Fill in the words vertically. (This puzzle does not make sense horizontally.)

This is a diagram of the cycle of materials in an ecosystem. Use the data from the pond community. How many members of each category can you find?

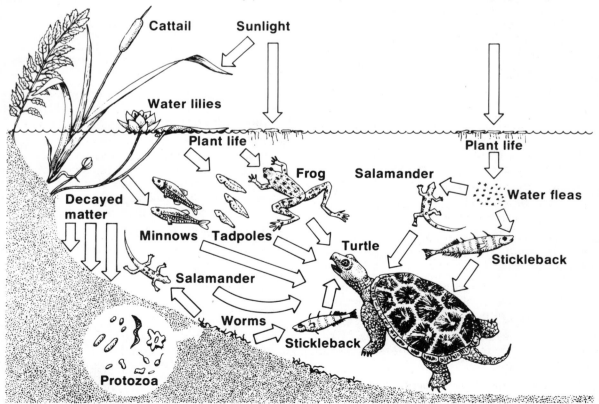

Cattail · Sunlight · Water lilies · Plant life · Frog · Salamander · Plant life · Water fleas · Decayed matter · Minnows · Tadpoles · Turtle · Stickleback · Salamander · Worms · Stickleback · Protozoa

## Using the World Is a Fresh Water Pond

Start students on the puzzle at upper left side of the ditto. The answers are:

### Answers to the Cycle Puzzle

| Producers | Consumers | Reducers | Environment |
|---|---|---|---|
| cattail | tadpoles | bacteria | water |
| plant life | minnows | fungi | dissolved materials |
| water lilies | stickleback | | temperature |
| | turtle | protozoa | light |
| | salamander | | |
| | water fleas | | |
| | worms | | |
| | frog | | |
| | protozoa | | |

While students are working on the puzzle, prepare to lead a discussion based on the following vocabulary. Don't give definitions away until you've received everybody's ideas.

**Ecology:** A branch of science concerned with the interaction of organisms and their environment. The key emphasis is on interrelationships. Ecology is defined by one scientist as the study of the total impact of man and other animals on the balance of nature.

**Ecosystem:** A functional system that includes the organisms of a natural community together with their environment.

**Community:** The animals and plants that, together with the environment, form the ecosystem. These organisms compete for food, water, and so on and reproduce if they can.

**Environment:** The physical surroundings in which the organisms of the community live. In the pond community, the environment is water, its dissolved material, and the climate.

**Energy:** Sunlight. Sunlight makes the ecosystem function. It is the force that causes the interactions to take place. The amount of energy that comes into the system determines the rate of productivity of the system. (See also the following definition concerning the effect of climate on productivity.)

**Productivity:** The rate at which energy is bound or matter combined into organic compounds by organisms, per unit time, per unit of the Earth's surface. Productivity in most communities is based wholly on the activities of green plants.

**Food chain:** Green plants use the energy of sunlight to produce organic substances from carbon dioxide and water. These plants are then eaten by animals, and these animals by other animals. Such a sequence of organisms is referred to as a food chain. (See also the following definition.)

**Food web:** Very much like the food chain, but it emphasizes the nonlinearity of the chains. (See the diagram on the ditto and also the following definition.)

**Cycling:** Of materials between organisms and the environment in the ecosystem.

**Producers:** The true, or green plants, which are nourished through photosynthesis.

**Consumers:** The animals that are characterized by their consumption or ingestion of organic food.

**Reducers:** Bacteria, fungi, saprobes, and other decomposers. They are characterized by their absorption of organic food and by their contribution to the breakdown of dead organic matter. See the diagram on the ditto, which shows the generalized relation among these last three items in the cycling of materials through the ecosystem.

### For discussion

Start the discussion with some questions like these: You've probably heard these words on TV and seen them in magazines. What do you think they mean? At this point, collect and accept all ideas students have about the meanings of these words. You might write these ideas on the blackboard as students express them. Then you might say, "After you have shared any ideas you have about the meanings of these words, we are going to explore the ditto together and some of the ideas involved there. When we finish, let's see if you have a clearer idea of what these terms are all about." (See hint 2 in Hints for Using the Materials in the Introduction.)

After you have explored the student's impressions of the meanings of the words in the vocabulary, call their attention to the picture of the pond community on the ditto. Most of the answers to the following questions can be abstracted by studying the picture. All the interrelationships are there.

## Exploratory Questions

Use these in any order you like . . . and in any quantity that you like.

1. What is the prime source of energy in this picture? *Answer:* sunlight

2. What do you think the environment of this community consists of? *Answer:* water and the materials dissolved in it, together with the climate which affects the temperature and light of the system.

3. Where do you think the plants in this community get their raw materials? *Answer:* air, water, mud and ooze at pond bottom, the droppings of birds and other animals, decayed matter of various sorts—all this together with the energy of sunlight.

4. How do you think the plant life of the pond is affected by the seasons and climate? *Answer:* When it gets colder, usually as the result of less sunlight, plant life dies off. The process of decay, by bacteria, occurs during winter. When the climate is tropical or subtropical, the processes of growth, death, decay, and new growth occurs all the time.

5. Where do the animals get their food? *Answer:* plants, or animals that feed on plants.

6. Where do the microscopic creatures live? *Answer:* Along the muddy bottom and undersides of larger plants are hundreds of thousands of single celled protozoa

7. What do these tiny creatures feed on? *Answer:* smaller protozoans or bacteria

8. What feeds on them? *Answer:* freshwater worms.

9. What else do freshwater worms feed on? *Answer:* rich bottom ooze full of decaying matter

10. What do the waterfleas eat? *Answer:* plant cells

11. What also eats plant cells? *Answer:* frogs, tadpoles, some kinds of fish, like minnows

12. What animals feed on the plant eaters that are animals? (see questions 10 and 11) *Answer:* sticklebacks, young salamanders, turtles

13. Look at the picture. Can you list some food chains? Here are some examples:

    sunlight→plant life→decayed matter→worms → stickleback → turtle

    sunlight → plant life → waterfleas →salamander → turtles

    decayed matter → protozoa → worms → stickleback → turtles

14. Ecologists sometimes refer to earth as Spaceship Earth. What do you think they mean by this? *Answer:* Earth's resources are finite and limited

15. One ecologist compares two types of economic organization of environmental resources: the cowboy economy and the spaceman economy. What do you think he means? **(Cowboy economy:** People used to think of the Earth as having limitless reservoirs of raw materials and endless areas for the deposit of wastes. For example, it was considered permissible to dump anything in the limitless ocean, even nerve gas. **Spaceman economy:** Today many people look upon both production and consumption with skepticism because they recognize that Earth's resources are limited. From this point of view it is considered desirable to slow down both production and consumption.)

# AFRICA OUT OF CONTEXT

Identify as many countries as you can—first without the map, then with.

Social Science

Class

Individuals

Dittos*

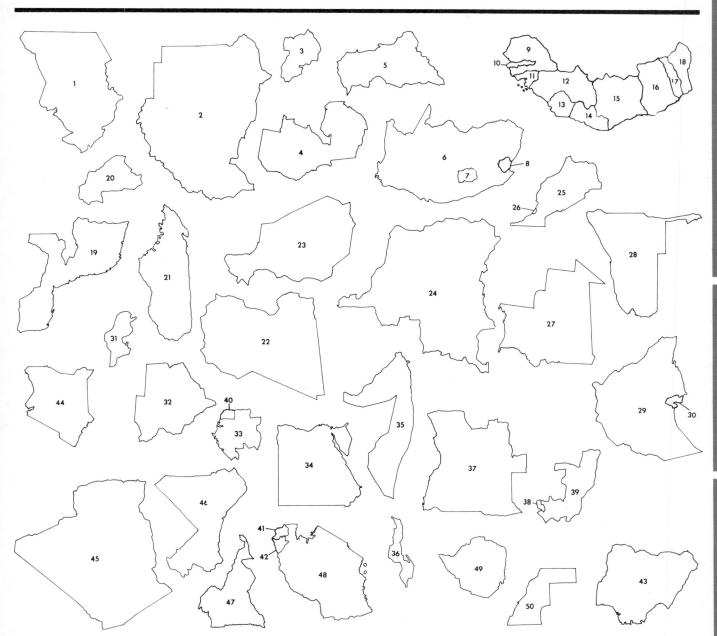

## Exploratory Questions about Africa

Without looking at a map of Africa:

1. How many countries can you see that would be neighbors on a map of Africa? Look at the shapes only. Look for shapes that would fit together. Write the numbers or names of the countries. After trying this exercise for a few moments, check your eyesight against the map.

2. See whether you can rate by size the ten *largest* African countries, simply by looking at the shapes. Write down the numbers from largest to smallest.

3. Can you tell which borders are on the ocean, again without looking at a map? Africa's borders are hard to distinguish because there are not many natural harbors and the shoreline is regular. But see what you can do. Later, check your results against the map.

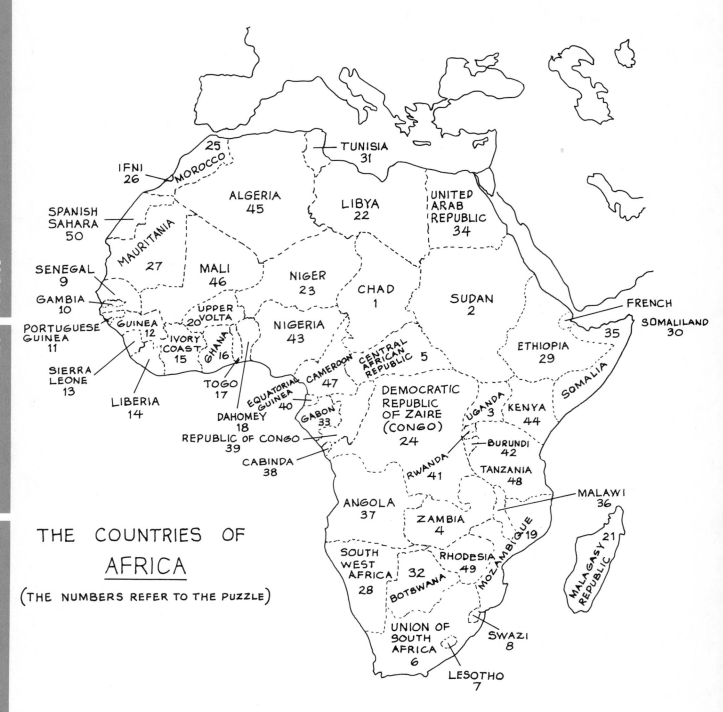

THE COUNTRIES OF

AFRICA

(THE NUMBERS REFER TO THE PUZZLE)

Social Studies

Class

Individuals

Dittos

With a map of Africa:

4. Historically, it has been very important for nations to have sea outlets. (Air transportation may have made seaports somewhat less important, but not significantly so.) Which of the large African nations have no access to the sea? Make a list. Pretend that you are predicting disputes for access to the sea. Where do you foresee trouble? Which countries would be aggressors against which defenders? Which countries are shaped in special ways simply to obtain an access to the sea? Judging by the layout of nations, where is the coastline the best in terms of having navigable seaports?

## Answers to Africa Out of Context

The map:

1. Chad
2. Sudan
3. Uganda
4. Zambia
5. Central African Republic
6. Union of South Africa
7. Lesotho
8. Swazi
9. Senegal
10. Gambia
11. Portuguese Guinea
12. Guinea
13. Sierra Leone
14. Liberia
15. Ivory Coast
16. Ghana
17. Togo
18. Dahomey
19. Mozambique
20. Upper Volta
21. Malagasy Republic
22. Libya
23. Niger
24. Democratic Republic of Zaire (Congo)
25. Morocco
26. Ifni
27. Mauritania
28. South West Africa
29. Ethiopia
30. French Somaliland
31. Tunisia
32. Botswana (Bechuanaland)
33. Gabon
34. United Arab Republic
35. Somalia
36. Malawi
37. Angola
38. Cabinda
39. Republic of the Congo
40. Equatorial Guinea
41. Rwanda
42. Burundi
43. Nigeria
44. Kenya
45. Algeria
46. Mali
47. Cameroon
48. Tanzania
49. Rhodesia
50. Spanish Sahara

## Answers to Exploratory Questions About Africa

Question 1:

No attempt is made here to write the complete list. Here are some sample answers. By looking at the shapes alone, hopefully some students will see that 1 (Chad) is south of 22 (Libya); that 46 (Mali) borders 27 (Mauritania) on the east and south; that 36 (Malawi) is north of 19 (Mozambique), etc.

Question 2: The ten largest African countries are:

1. Sudan (2) ·················· 967,501 square miles
2. Algeria (45) ················ 919,593 square miles
3. Congo (24) ················ 905,565 square miles
4. Libya (22) ················· 679,360 square miles
5. Chad (1) ·················· 495,754 square miles
6. Niger (23) ················· 489,190 square miles
7. Angola (37) ················ 481,352 square miles
8. South Africa (6) ··········· 471,446 square miles
9. Mali (46) ·················· 463,949 square miles
10. Ethiopia (29) ··············· 457,267 square miles

Question 3:

This question is hard to answer. Students should look for irregular borders, islands, or many small countries clustered closely (each possibly seeking a water border). Examples: The countries numbered 9 through 18 are all clustered in one direction, to the south. Further clue here, 11 has islands south of it. Thus, it is a fair bet that these countries border on water. Area 48 has islands.

Other than these examples, it is probably impossible to tell other water boundaries since Africa has few islands and a very regular coastline.

Question 4:

(With a map of Africa). The large African nations with no sea access are: Botswana (Bechuanaland), Central African Republic, Chad, Mali, Niger, Rhodesia, Upper Volta, Zambia.

The students' predictions about possible future trouble spots would vary. Countries which are shaped in special ways to obtain an access to the sea include Zaire (its western border).

Because the west coast of Africa is lined with small nations, each hugging the shore, this could be judged to be the best shoreline. Remember, however, there may be other historical reasons why there are so many countries there. The map can only lead to a guess here.

Looking at all the countries, 36 African nations have a sea access, 14 do not. So it's fair to say that, in general, most countries are shaped to have a sea access.

Social Studies

Class

Individuals

Social Studies Science

Class

Individuals

Dittos

**ADOBE OF CLAY AND GRASS**

1 to 5 stories high. Up to 200 families.

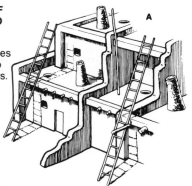

A

B

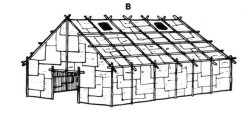

**ELM BARK AND LOGS**   50 to 100 feet long.
6 to 10 families.

C

**SOD EARTH**

30 to 40 feet diameter.
40 to 60 people.

**ELM BARK GRASS**

1 to 3 families.

D

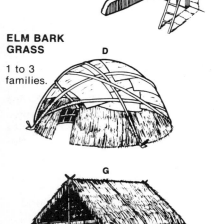

**PINE POLES BUFFALO HIDES**

1 family

E

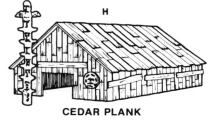

F

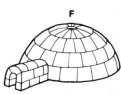

**ICE AND SNOW**

1 to 3 familes.

G

**GRASS (OPEN)**

H

**CEDAR PLANK**

40 to 50 families.

I

**GRASS AND POLES**

40 to 60 persons.

|   | Nomad or settled? | Rain: Large amounts, little, none? | Climate: Warm, hot or cold? | Trees: Large, small or none? | Mainly farmers hunters, fishermen or gatherers? |
|---|---|---|---|---|---|
| A |   |   |   |   |   |
| B |   |   |   |   |   |
| C |   |   |   |   |   |
| D |   |   |   |   |   |
| E |   |   |   |   |   |
| F |   |   |   |   |   |
| G |   |   |   |   |   |
| H |   |   |   |   |   |
| I |   |   |   |   |   |

## Anthro: Homes

**Object:** To give students a chance to be amateur anthropologists. To permit them to form as many ideas and conclusions from picture data as their imaginations permit.

**Student groupings:** Individuals or small groups.

**Procedure:** The pictures on the students' page show nine distinct homes used by various tribes of American Indians in the past. Students are to use the pictures to fill in as much of the chart as possible. They should use the pictures and the information given to draw conclusions or to make educated guesses. Let them work alone or in small groups.

It is important to remember that the purpose is not simply to obtain the correct answers but to let students work like anthropologists, drawing conclusions from physical, nonverbal data.

After the students have worked on the chart for a while, discuss it with them. Which cells of the chart were filled in most easily? Which were hardest to do? Do these pictures give other categories of information? Most likely, you'll find some disagreements in the way the charts were filled in. That's fine. You'll also find that these pictures do not give all the information needed to make firm conclusions. After all, houses are only one of many sources of evidence about the tribes.

Not only do houses not provide conclusive evidence but in some cases they might provide misleading evidence. Take the case of the Northwest plank house. One might think this was found in an agricultural region because there were probably large trees and heavy rainfall. However, this was a special region with such a rich supply of fish (mainly salmon) that people never had to farm to obtain food. Fishing and food-gathering provided an abundance of food. Indians in this region even had time for the arts—note the decoration on the house and the tall totem pole! Do not be discouraged by exceptions like this one! They are what make anthropology so intriguing! Our hope is that this exercise will raise questions in students' minds that they will seek to answer later.

### Identification of the homes on student page

The tribes listed are representative. Others in the area used similar homes.

**A.** Southwest Pueblo adobe apartment house (Pueblo Indians). Still in use

**B.** Northeast woodlands long house (Iroquois Indians)

**C.** Central plains earth lodge (Mandan Indians)

**D.** Northeast woodlands wigwam (Algonquian Indians)

**E.** Central plains tepee (Blackfoot Indians)

**F.** Arctic domed snowhouse, igloo (Eskimos)

**G.** Southeast woodlands thatched summer house (Seminole Indians)

**H.** Northwest plank house (Tlingit Indians)

**I.** California thatched house (Yuma Indians)

### Answers

Here is a copy of the chart with *suggested* answers. Be flexible with the answers. There will be a great deal of overlapping.

| | Nomad or settled? | Rain: a large amount, little, none? | Climate: warm, hot, cold? | Trees: large, small, none? | *Mainly* farmers, hunters, fishermen, gatherers? |
|---|---|---|---|---|---|
| A | Settled | Little or none. Elaborate irrigation system still in use. | Hot and cold | Small | *Farmers*— large community |
| B | Settled | Large amount | Hot and cold | Large | *Farmers, hunters, gatherers* |
| C | Settled probably | Little or none | Hot and cold | Small or none | *Hunters, gatherers, farmers. Food scarce, tried everything* |
| D | Settled | Large amount | Hot and cold | Large | *Farmers, hunters, gatherers* |
| E | Nomad | Little | Hot and cold | Small or none. The poles for tepee were dragged by dogs from place to place | *Hunters, gatherers* |
| F | Settled— had different passages for summer and winter. | Snow, large amount of rain | Cold | None | *Hunters* |
| G | Settled | Large amount | Hot | Large | *Farmers* |
| H | Settled | Large amount | Hot and cold | Large | *Fishermen, gatherers. Looks like farming area— but is not. (See discussion note.)* |
| I | Settled | Large amount | Warm to hot | Small | *Gatherers, fishermen, farmers* |

# Cities Go, Cities Grow

Here are two puzzles dealing with the largest American cities. One is based on the 1950 census; the other on the 1970 census. Think of cities that will fit in the *vertical* letter boxes. (The puzzle makes no sense horizontally.) The numbers above and below each city show its rank in the census. Some city names and ranks stayed the same over the twenty years. Some were surprisingly different. You'll see!

1950

1970

What can we learn from these puzzles? You might try perhaps to arrange the two lists of cities in proper rank for easier reading and evaluation.

Which cities disappeared from the top fifteen between 1950 and 1970? There are four. _____

Which cities appeared in the 1970 list but not in the 1950 list? There are four. _____

How many cities in California were in the 1950 list? the 1970 list? _____

How many cities in Texas were in the 1950 list? the 1970 list? _____

How many cities in New York were in the 1950 list? the 1970 list? _____

Which cities fell in the ratings? There were eight. _____

Which cities rose in the ratings? There were seven. _____

Which cities remained the same? There are four. _____

What conclusions do you draw from your work? How might rankings change if we included suburban areas? Discuss this.

## Answers to *Cities Go, Cities Grow*

Largest cities:

| The order for 1950: | The order for 1970: |
|---|---|
| 1. New York | 1. New York |
| 2. Chicago | 2. Chicago |
| 3. Philadelphia | 3. Los Angeles |
| 4. Los Angeles | 4. Philadelphia |
| 5. Detroit | 5. Detroit |
| 6. Baltimore | 6. Houston |
| 7. Cleveland | 7. Baltimore |
| 8. St. Louis | 8. Dallas |
| 9 Washington, D. C. | 9. Washington, D. C. |
| 10. Boston | 10. Cleveland |
| 11. San Francisco | 11. Indianapolis |
| 12. Pittsburgh | 12. Milwaukee |
| 13. Milwaukee | 13. San Francisco |
| 14. Houston | 14. San Diego |
| 15. Buffalo | 15. San Antonio |

**Note:** The growth (or lack of it) of the city itself does not always reflect the growth of the metropolitan area of which it is the center. The census figures for metropolitan areas vary from the ones given here.

Cities that disappeared from the top fifteen between 1950 and 1970: St. Louis, Boston, Pittsburgh, and Buffalo. (All, but St. Louis, are east of the Mississippi River.)

Cities that appeared in the 1970 list, but not the 1950 list: Dallas, Indianapolis, San Diego, and San Antonio. (All but Indianapolis are west of the Mississippi River.)

In 1950, two cities in California were on the list; in 1970, three cities were.

In 1950, one city in Texas was on the list; in 1970, three cities were.

In 1950, two cities in New York were on the list; in 1970, one city was.

Cities that fell in the rankings: Philadelphia, Baltimore, Cleveland, St. Louis, Boston, San Francisco, Pittsburgh, and Buffalo. (All but San Francisco are east of the Mississippi River.)

Cities that rose in the rankings: Los Angeles, Houston, Dallas, Indianapolis, Milwaukee, San Diego, San Antonio. (All but Indianapolis and Milwaukee are west of the Mississippi River.)

Cities that remained the same in the ratings: New York, Chicago, Detroit, and Washington, D. C. (All are east of the Mississippi River.)

In discussing the growth and decline of cities, remember that recently the largest growth of population has been in the suburbs. Figures for suburbs are *not* included here. Thus, it is likely that some cities that declined in the rankings may be the center of rapidly growing suburban areas.

# EUROPE OUT OF CONTEXT

*The countries of Europe are shown in the right shapes and relative size. See how many of these you can recognize, first without using a map, and then using one.*

## Exploratory Questions about Europe

Without looking at a map of Europe:

1. Some European countries are obviously on a sea or an ocean. Which ones are these? Why is this obvious?

2. What statements can you make about Europe simply by looking at the shapes? Statements can be about size, position, number of countries, and so on. Let your imagination roam!

With the map of Europe:

3. The history of Europe has long been influenced by the struggle to gain access to the sea (to have a seaport). Which countries made it? Which didn't? That is, which countries are landlocked? Which countries have access to a small sea but must pass through a narrow channel that is controlled by another country to get out to a large sea or an ocean? Which countries have open access to a large sea or an ocean? Which countries control important channels?

4. What conclusions can you draw from your observations? Many more questions can be asked. Think up your own questions.

## Answers to *Europe Out of Context*

1. Italy
2. France
3. Portugal
4. Sweden
5. Greece
6. Romania
7. Finland
8. The Netherlands
9. Albania
10. Denmark
11. Switzerland
12. Austria
13. West Germany
14. East Germany
15. Great Britain
16. Ireland
17. Northern Ireland
18. Union of Soviet Socialist Republics (U.S.S.R.)
19. Belgium
20. Hungary
21. Yugoslavia
22. Bulgaria
23. Poland
24. Luxembourg
25. Czechoslovakia
26. Spain
27. Norway
28. Iceland

## Answers to Exploratory Questions About Europe

1. The countries obviously having water borders are those with islands. There are about eleven of these.

3. 

| Landlocked nations | Access to a small sea | Access to open seas | | Control of channels: |
|---|---|---|---|---|
| Austria | East Germany | Albania | Netherlands | England (English Channel and Gibraltar) |
| Czechoslovakia | Bulgaria | Belgium | Northern | France (English Channel) |
| Hungary | Finland | Denmark | Ireland | Denmark (Kattegat and Skagerrak) |
| Luxembourg | Poland | France | Norway | Spain (around Gibraltar) |
| Switzerland | Romania | Great | Portugal | Turkey (Bosporus, access to Aegean, Mediterranean seas) |
| | U.S.S.R. | Britain | Spain | |
| | | Greece | Sweden | |
| | | Iceland | West | |
| | | Italy | Germany | |
| | | Ireland | Yugoslavia | |

**Note:** There may be some discussion or disagreement about definitions. What is a small sea? What is access to open seas? Such discussion is good. Encourage it!

# FREE US! We're sentenced!

Hidden in each of the sentences below is the name of a state. To find it, connect letters from two or more words. Circle the states you find.

Example: The ra(dio wa)s broken, so we took it to the shop.

1. He had to color a door and chimney before the picture was finished.

2. "Are you ill?" I noisily asked the old man, before I realized he could not hear me.

3. It was but a hut in the woods, but to us it was heaven!

4. Did a hole in the street puncture your tire?

5. Oh, I only meant it as a ridiculous joke!

6. Our friend took us in his private plane, and we flew over Monticello.

7. We seem to face a dilemma in everything we do.

8. A lab amateur ruined the experiment for all the old-timers.

9. The grateful man beamed and said, "Al, ask anything you want!"

10. Right here, in Diana's room is an intricate spider's web.

Now see if you can find the hidden U.S. president in each sentence below. One sentence has two.

1. When he smoked a cigar Thursday, he burned a hole in the sofa.

2. Robert invited Mary, Ken, Ned, Yolanda, and Alice to his cottage.

3. Every time I see him, I wonder why is Jack so naughty.

4. What! After all I've been through! I have to go swimming again?

5. The dog ran toward the pier certainly without thinking about falling in the water.

6. The truck dumped land fill, more than we'll ever be able to use.

7. The new style resembled the flappers of the 1920s.

8. What rum and gin was sold already?

Finally, here are a few countries of the whole world to test your skill!

1. He had taken yards of the material before the theft was discovered.

2. They always traveled to a health spa in the high mountains.

3. The sniper underestimated the policeman's fire.

**STATES**

**PRESIDENTS**

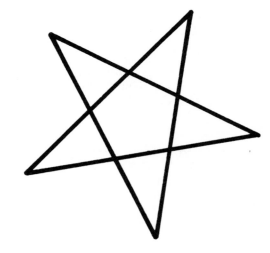

**COUNTRIES**

Now it's your turn! Make up some of these sentences. It's fun!

140

**Answers to *Free Us! We're Sentenced!***

*States*

1. color a door
2. ill I noisily
3. but a hut
4. did a hole
5. oh I only
6. over Monticello
7. dilemma in everything
8. a lab amateur
9. Al ask anything
10. in Diana's

*Presidents*

1. cigar Thursday
2. Ken Ned Yolanda
3. Jack so nervous
4. what after
5. pier certainly     dog ran toward
6. fill more
7. style resembles
8. what rum and

*Countries*

1. taken yards
2. spa in
3. sniper underestimated

# Games & Fields

Here are the playing fields or courts of eighteen popular sports and games (not drawn to scale). Can you recognize them? Write the names in the spaces given.

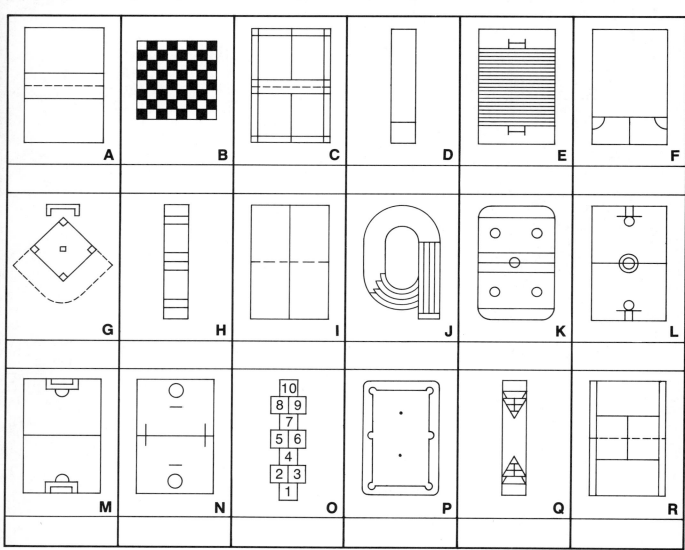

**Discussion Questions:** Use reference books to obtain answers, if you like.

1. If these diagrams were drawn to scale, which would be the largest? smallest? How would you rank these sport and game-playing areas, from largest to smallest?

2. How many of these games are played with a ball? Which ones?

3. In how many of these sports is an instrument, other than parts of the body, used to handle the ball? In which ones?

4. Which of these games have one player per team? (There are five games.) Which have one or two per side? (There are five games.) Which have five? (There is one game.) Which have six? (There are two games.) Which have nine? (There is one game.) Which have ten? (There is one game.) Which have eleven? (There are two games.)

142

## Answers to Games and Fields

The games are:

A—volleyball
B—checkers, chess
C—badminton
D—bowling
E—football
F—squash
G—baseball
H—fencing
I —table tennis (ping-pong)
J—track

K —ice hockey
L —basketball
M—soccer
N—lacrosse
O—hopscotch
P—pocket billiards (pool)
Q—shuffleboard
R—tennis

1. The largest playing field is for track; the smallest for chess.

The fields, from largest to smallest are:

| | |
|---|---|
| track | 100,000 square feet (approx.) |
| soccer | 81,000 square feet |
| baseball | 75,000 square feet |
| lacrosse | 69,300 square feet |
| football | 57,000 square feet |
| ice hockey | 17,000 square feet |
| basketball | 4,700 square feet |
| tennis | 2,106 square feet (singles) |
| volleyball | 1,800 square feet |
| badminton | 880 square feet |
| squash | 592 square feet (singles) |
| shuffleboard | 312 square feet |
| bowling | 266 square feet |
| fencing | 240 square feet |
| hopscotch | court varies |
| ping-pong | 45 square feet |
| pool | 36 square feet (approx.) |
| chess | board varies |

2. Eleven sports are played with a ball. They are baseball, basketball, bowling, football, lacrosse, ping-pong, pool, soccer, squash, tennis, volleyball.

3. In six, an instrument is used to handle the ball. They are baseball, lacrosse, ping-pong, pool, squash, tennis.

4. Number of players per team or side:

one player: bowling, chess, fencing, pool, track, hopscotch

one or two players: badminton, ping-pong, shuffleboard, squash, tennis

five players: basketball

six players: ice hockey, volleyball

nine players: baseball

ten players: lacrosse

eleven players: football, soccer

## Open-ended Discussion Questions

1. You can easily design a mini-survey to find out which sports are the favorites among the class members. Make a chart of them, showing the names of the sports and the numbers of students who like them best. Sports could be divided into those students like to play (participant) and those they like to watch (spectator). Of course, one student's participant favorite could be another's spectator favorite. Here's a chart model:

| Games | Participant favorite | Spectator favorite |
|---|---|---|
| badminton chess | (write number ↓ of students) | (write number ↓ of students) |

2. Do you know where or when some of these games started? The origins of many games (such as chess, football, fencing, soccer, and tennis) are disputed because they go back so far in history. Many nations claim to have originated them. Yet, the following games can be traced to a definite place and a not-so-definite time. Discuss.

badminton—India, ancient

basketball—U.S.A., 1891

bowling—Germany, ancient

ice hockey—Canada, 1870's

lacrosse—Canadian Indians, ancient

3. What makes a good game or sport? Such aspects as skill, luck, conflict, excitement, and timing, will undoubtedly be mentioned. What elements are common to all (or most) sports and games? Students may find that they disagree among themselves about the attributes of specific games.

# Hidden Black Leaders

The last names of famous black Americans (both of today and yesterday) are hidden in the square below. Look for them, up, down, across, backwards, sideways, all ways! Circle them as you find them.

Which names would you add? Who are the leaders of today and tomorrow?

Social Studies — Individuals — Dittos

| B | Y | E | V | R | A | G | B | I | L | E | K | G | T | D | W |
|---|---|---|---|---|---|---|---|---|---|---|---|---|---|---|---|
| B | C | N | I | L | K | N | A | R | F | L | I | N | U | L | A |
| A | N | D | E | R | S | O | N | N | E | L | N | U | R | E | S |
| L | W | E | A | V | E | R | F | W | O | I | G | O | N | I | H |
| I | D | A | N | H | I | T | N | G | O | S | R | Y | E | F | I |
| D | J | O | W | E | N | S | I | A | H | O | K | E | R | R | N |
| A | I | S | A | M | X | M | C | M | M | N | D | C | T | A | G |
| V | S | W | I | X | P | R | B | O | B | B | K | S | A | W | T |
| I | S | R | L | O | X | A | X | Y | T | U | U | M | O | J | O |
| S | A | I | E | N | B | X | R | X | E | T | T | T | O | N | N |
| I | L | G | U | V | O | U | L | K | S | N | I | K | L | I | W |
| U | G | H | S | P | E | L | D | J | O | H | N | S | O | N | Q |
| O | U | T | R | H | A | N | S | B | E | R | R | Y | D | O | T |
| L | O | S | E | H | I | H | U | G | H | E | S | L | T | U | Y |
| V | D | N | S | W | E | N | S | S | W | C | A | R | V | E | R |
| X | A | R | D | I | C | I | I | P | A | R | K | S | L | L | J |
| J | A | L | L | H | V | R | J | O | E | E | C | I | R | P | A |
| M | A | U | E | A | X | M | L | O | C | L | A | M | Z | Z | N |
| B | J | Y | D | D | Z | Z | Z | R | O | B | I | N | S | O | N |

## You should have found:

Anderson (Marian)
Ali (Muhammed)
Armstrong (Louis)
Bailey (Pearl)
Baldwin (James)
Bunche (Ralph)
Carver (George W.)
Davis (Ossie)
Davis (Sammy, Jr.)
Douglass (Frederick)
DuBois (W. E. B.)

Ellison (Ralph)
Evers (Charles)
Franklin (John Hope)
Garvey (Marcus)
Hansberry (Lorraine)
Hughes (Langston)
Jackson (Mahalia)
Johnson (John E.)
King (Martin Luther, Jr.)
Louis (Joe)
Malcolm X

Marshall (Thurgood)
Parks (Rosa)
Price (Leontyne)
Owens (Jesse)
Robinson (Jackie)
Scott (Dred)
Tubman (Harriet)
Turner (Nat)
Warfield (William)
Washington (Booker T.)
Weaver (Robert C.)

Wilkins (Roy)
Woodson (Carter G.)
Wright (Richard)
Young (Whitney, Jr.)

1. Who are the two black Nobel Prize winners?
2. Who was the first black in professional baseball?
3. Who is the publisher of *Ebony, Jet, Negro Digest* and other magazines?
4. Who was the "father of Negro history"?
5. Who was the first black Supreme Court justice?

**Answers to *Hidden Black Leaders***

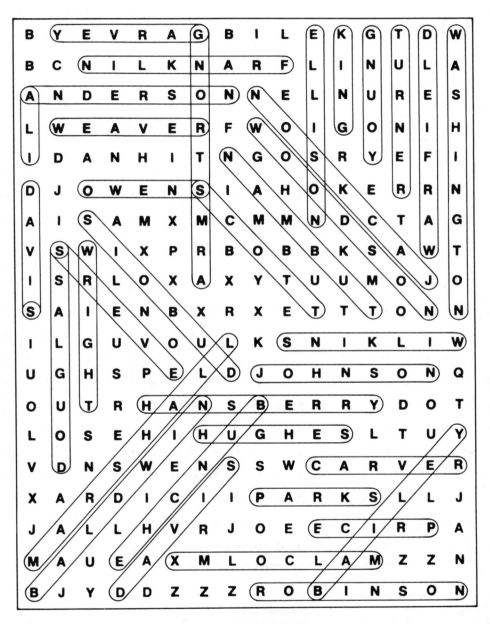

1. The two Nobel Peace Prize winners were Ralph Bunche and Martin Luther King, Jr.

2. The first black in professional baseball was Jackie Robinson (1947).

3. The publisher of *Ebony, Jet,* etc. is John E. Johnson.

4. The "father of Negro history" was Carter G. Woodson.

5. The first black Supreme Court Justice was Thurgood Marshall.

# Hidden States

The fifty states are hidden in the letter square. Look down, up, backwards, diagonally, sideways, all directions! Circle them as you find them.

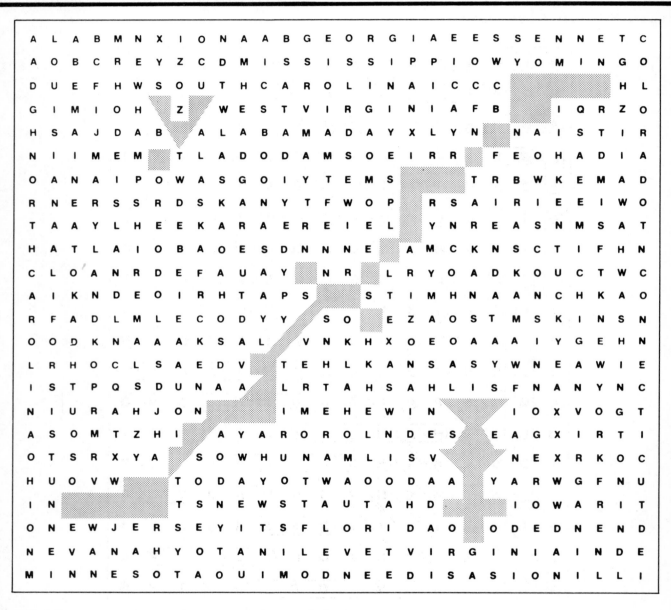

```
A L A B M N X I O N A A B G E O R G I A E E S S E N N E T C
A O B C R E Y Z C D M I S S I S S I P P I O W Y O M I N G O
D U E F H W S O U T H C A R O L I N A I C C C         H L
G I M I O H Z W E S T V I R G I N I A F B         I Q R Z O
H S A J D A B A L A B A M A D A Y X L Y N   N A I S T I R
N I I M E M   T L A D O D A M S O E I R R   F E O H A D I A
O A N A I P O W A S G O I Y T E M S       T R B W K E M A D
R N E R S S R D S K A N Y T F W O P   R S A I R I E E I W O
T A A Y L H E E K A R A E R E I E L   Y N R E A S N M S A T
H A T L A I O B A O E S D N N N E   A M C K N S C T I F H N
C L O A N R D E F A U A Y     N R   L R Y O A D K O U C T W C
A I K N D E O I R H T A P S   S T I M H N A A N C H K A O
R F A D L M L E C O D Y Y   S O   E Z A O S T M S K I N S N
O O D K N A A A K S A L   V N K H X O E O A A A I Y G E H N
L R H O C L S A E D V   T E H L K A N S A S Y W N E A W I E
I S T P Q S D U N A A   L R T A H S A H L I S F N A N Y N C
N I U R A H J O N   I M E H E W I N     I O X V O G T
A S O M T Z H I   A Y A R O R O L N D E S   E A G X I R T I
O T S R X Y A   S O W H U N A M L I S V   N E X R K O C
H U O V W   T O D A Y O T W A O O D A A   Y A R W G F N U
I N     T S N E W S T A U T A H D   I O W A R I T
O N E W J E R S E Y I T S F L O R I D A O   O D E D N E N D
N E V A N A H Y O T A N I L E V E T V I R G I N I A I N D E
M I N N E S O T A O U I M O D N E E D I S A S I O N I L L I
```

## List of states

| | | | | | |
|---|---|---|---|---|---|
| Alabama | Georgia | Maine | Nevada | Oregon | Virginia |
| Alaska | Hawaii | Maryland | New Hampshire | Pennsylvania | Washington |
| Arizona | Idaho | Massachusetts | New Jersey | Rhode Island | West Virginia |
| Arkansas | Illinois | Michigan | New Mexico | South Carolina | Wisconsin |
| California | Indiana | Minnesota | New York | South Dakota | Wyoming |
| Colorado | Iowa | Mississippi | North Carolina | Tennessee | |
| Connecticut | Kansas | Missouri | North Dakota | Texas | |
| Delaware | Kentucky | Montana | Ohio | Utah | |
| Florida | Louisiana | Nebraska | Oklahoma | Vermont | |

Social Studies

Individuals

Dittos

## Answers to *Hidden States*

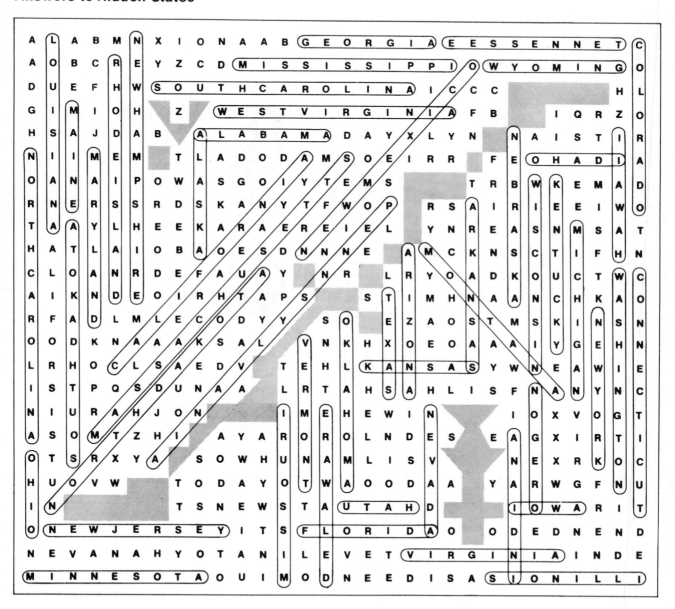

# PROCEED WITH CAUTION!

The U.S. is going international!
Have you noticed our road signs are changing?

By 1975, our road signs will be patterned after the international road sign system. Today, we will experiment with the new signs. Let's see if these signs are easy to decipher. Can you figure out the system? Let's try to make our own signs conform to the new system.

First, how easy are the new signs to decode? Here are fifteen signs, in the old form and in the new. Can you match the pairs that deliver the same message?

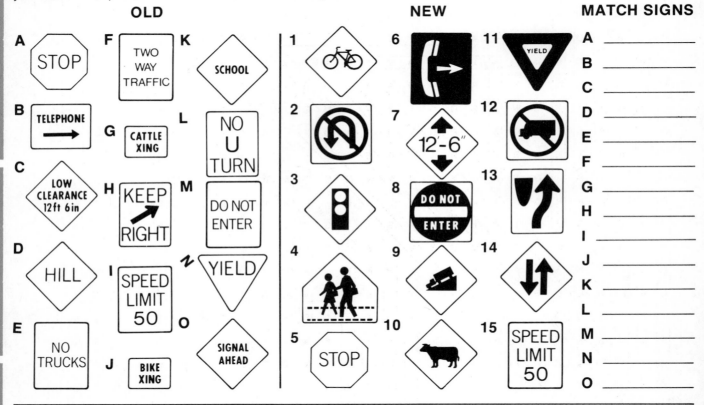

| OLD | NEW | MATCH SIGNS |

A _____
B _____
C _____
D _____
E _____
F _____
G _____
H _____
I _____
J _____
K _____
L _____
M _____
N _____
O _____

Finally, let's see whether we can make up our own signs, using the new system. Here are eight of the old signs. Draw your version of these signs as you think they might appear in the new system. (The teacher's page shows them—you can compare after you've given it a try.)

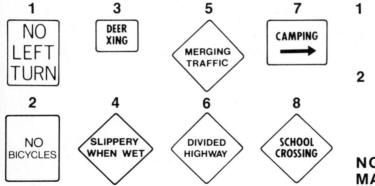

1    3    5    7

2    4    6    8

**NOW—ON YOUR WAY HOME—SEE HOW MANY OF THE NEW SIGNS YOU FIND...**

148

## Answers to the Matching Puzzle, *Proceed With Caution*

A—5
B—6
C—7
D—9
E—12
F—14
G—10
H—13
I—15
J—1
K—4
L—2
M—8
N—11
O—3

## Part II

### For discussion

Ask these questions after students have done the matching exercise.

1. How did you do? How many could you match? Were the new signs clear? Which were matched correctly most frequently? least frequently? Why?

2. What is the basic difference between the old and new signs? (Class should see that the new ones have more pictures and symbols.)

3. Which signs remain the same in both the old and new systems? (stop, speed limit) Why do you suppose these did not change? (They were clear already.)

4. Why are new signs being adopted? What advantages do they have? (Among other responses, students should understand that the symbol and picture signs facilitate international travel. It is easier to drive in foreign countries if road signs are not in a foreign language. Also, symbols, once understood, are easier to read and react to in a flash second of time than are words, and this may be crucial on the road.)

5. Why was the U.S. slow to adopt these signs? Europe has been using them for a long time, as have many nations all over the world. The system of international road signs was worked out in 1949, in a project sponsored by the United Nations. (Pos-

sible answers: We had a well-developed sign system (better than Europe's) and did not wish to switch over. We are a large nation off by ourselves, removed by water from most other countries. Travel here is not similar to travel in Europe. There, the motorist can drive from one country to another within a relatively short distance. There are approximately sixty languages in Europe. Our isolationist tendencies may have played a role.)

## Part III

Let's discuss the shapes of the signs. These shapes are crucial to their meanings. What shapes are used? Tell the class, or ask them to study their papers and tell you. Draw the shapes on the board, as shown in the following.

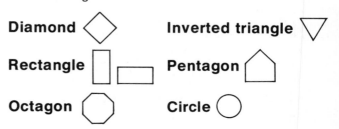

When students have the signs in front of them, help them discover what the shapes symbolize. Each shape has a general category of meaning, such as prohibition, warning, instruction, etc.

You and the class should discover meanings of the shapes:

**Diamond** ◇ warning

**Rectangle** ▯ ▭ traffic regulation / guidance information

**Octagon** ⯃ stop

**Pennant** ▷ (not used in this lesson) no passing zone

**Inverted Triangle** ▽ yield

**Pentagon**  **school**

**Circle** ◯ **railroad crossing (not used here)**

Color, also, is significant in the new signs. In the following, you will find the colors of the actual signs and the meanings of each. Have the class analyze the colors that the signs shown on their papers will actually be.

| | |
|---|---|
| red: | stop, prohibition (do not!) |
| green: | movement permitted, directional guidance |
| blue: | motorist services |
| yellow: | general warning |
| black on white: | regulation signs |
| orange: | construction, maintenance warnings |
| brown: | public recreation and scenic guidance |

Compare the class's findings with this guide:

red: stop (5), do not enter (8), no trucks (12), no U turn (2), Yield (11).

green:

Blue: telephone (6).

yellow: school (4), hill (9), keep right (13), bike xing (1), two way traffic (14), low clearance (7), cattle xing (10), signal ahead (3)

black on white: speed limit (15).

orange:

brown:

### Part IV

Finally, have the class do Part IV on their ditto papers. Again, compare their drawings with the signs in the new system. Answers: ditto

**1**  **2**  **3**  **4**

**5** **6** **7** **8**

The class should have a good idea of whether the new signs are clear and distinct. Hopefully, they will be more aware of them and the system according to which they were designed.

# Scrambled Cities U.S.A.

Here's a three-part puzzle:

1. Unscramble the cities. Write the correct name under the scrambled one.
2. Write the states that the cities are in. Cities are grouped in two's and three's. (If you know the state before you can unscramble all the cities, that will help you!)
3. Circle the city if it is a state capital. (Clue: Eleven are.)

| States | | Cities | | |
|--------|-----|--------|--------|--------|
| | 1. fablouf | ronkwye | | resyacus |
| *Kansas* *Wichita* | 2. achiitw | | akpote *Topeka* | |
| | 3. sheatalleas | aimim | | begsterpturs |
| | 4. hippidalealh | | hiptsrgubt | |
| | 5. patredovn | midessone | | xitosciuy |
| | 6. gidefsrinpl | | soonbt | |
| | 7. dadparisnrg | nnagils | | teirodt |
| | 8. gosellosan | | rissannafocc | |
| | 9. shotuno | sdalal | | lapeos |
| | 10. tebtu | | gliblisn | |
| | 11. robotaugen | wenalsroen | | verotehpsr |
| | 12. krawen | | yticcitlanta | |
| | 13. revned | lobpue | | snigprsodraoclo |
| | 14. balocumi | | leastonrhc | |
| | 15. egarohcna | raksifban | | eajnuu |
| | 16. tulhud | silopaennim | | tuslap |
| | 17. gidefsrinpl | rocia | | ogacihc |

## Answers to Scrambled U.S. Cities

| States | Cities (Underlined ones are state capitals) |
|--------|---------------------------------------------|
| 1. New York | Buffalo, New York, Syracuse |
| 2. Kansas | Wichita, <u>Topeka</u> |
| 3. Florida | Tallahassee, Miami, St. Petersburg |
| 4. Pennsylvania | Philadelphia, Pittsburgh |
| 5. Iowa | Davenport, <u>Des Moines</u>, Sioux City |
| 6. Massachusetts | Springfield, <u>Boston</u> |
| 7. Michigan | Grand Rapids, <u>Lansing</u>, Detroit |
| 8. California | Los Angeles, San Francisco |
| 9. Texas | Houston, Dallas, El Paso |
| 10. Montana | Butte, Billings |
| 11. Louisiana | <u>Baton Rouge</u>, New Orleans, Shreveport |
| 12. New Jersey | Newark, Atlantic City |
| 13. Colorado | <u>Denver</u>, Pueblo, Colorado Springs |
| 14. South Carolina | <u>Columbia</u>, Charleston |
| 15. Alaska | Anchorage, Fairbanks, <u>Juneau</u> |
| 16. Minnesota | Duluth, Minneapolis, <u>St. Paul</u> |
| 17. Illinois | <u>Springfield</u>, Cairo, Chicago |

# STOP! YOU'RE UNDER ARREST!

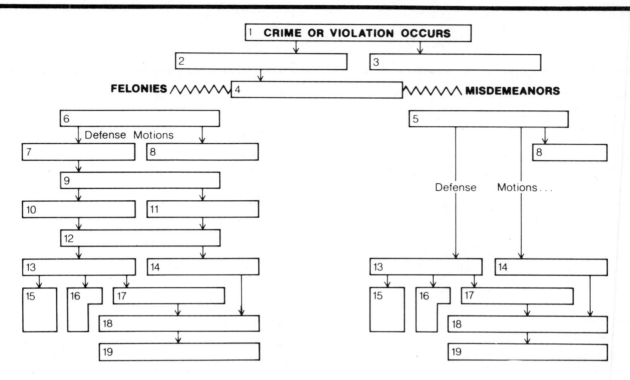

**The Procedure** (in alphabetical order):

**Acquittal:** defendant is found not guilty.

**Arraignment of suspect (in misdemeanor cases):** suspect is told the charges against him, is given right to get a lawyer, can plead guilty or innocent, bail is set, trial date is set.

**Arraignment of suspect (in felony cases):** (a) *preliminary arraignment:* suspect is told the charges against him, is given right to get a lawyer, bail is set, preliminary hearing date is set. (b) *felony arraignment:* charge against defendant is made after the indictment, bail is set, defendant can plead innocent or guilty.

**Arrest:** police investigate the crime and arrest suspect; seek information about the crime, use search and arrest warrants.

**Booking of suspect:** suspect's name and the charge against him are written in police records; he is fingerprinted and photographed.

**Charge dismissed:** person is freed of charge against him.

**Conviction:** defendant is found guilty.

**Defense motions:** defendant and attorney try to suppress evidence, throw out confessions, get lab tests, compel evidence for the defendant, get a sanity hearing, and so on.

**Grand jury:** in felony cases, meets in secret to see if there is enough evidence against suspect to indict him (see indictment below).

**Guilty plea:** defendant admits charge against him.

**Hung jury:** jurors in petit jury cannot agree on a verdict.

**Indictment:** in felony cases, formal accusation, stating the crime and the facts about it, usually presented by a grand jury.

**No bill:** in felony cases, finding by grand jury that there is not enough evidence for a formal accusation; charges are dismissed.

**Preliminary hearing:** in felony cases, prosecution presents first outline of case against defendant; judge evaluates if there is enough evidence to hold defendant for the grand jury.

**Presentence investigation:** to determine best sentence for the convicted person; conducted by probation department.

**Sentencing:** punishment is set for convict.

**Suspect not caught or not found or released:** for various reasons, by police or other official.

**Trial:** held in court in front of judge or petit jury to determine guilt or innocence of defendant; the decision is called a verdict.

## Directions for Class in *Stop! You're Under Arrest*

**Give these directions to the class:** What is the step-by-step procedure from 1 to 19? Here is a chart showing criminal procedure. It awaits your completion. Use the definitions given to fill in each slot. Note the parallel numbering in the felony and misdemeanor procedures when the same steps occur in both.

Here are some more words the class will probably need to do this activity. Go over them before the students start on the charts or while they are doing them.

1. **suspect:** person suspected of a crime, before formal charges are brought against him.

2. **defendant:** person against whom a charge is brought in court.

3. **convict:** person found guilty of a crime and serving a prison sentence.

4. **prosecutor:** person who brings charges against the defendant in court on behalf of the government.

5. **grand jury:** jurors, usually twenty-three, who decide whether there is enough evidence to try a person. If so, they issue an indictment; if not, a no bill. They meet in secret.

6. **petit jury:** jurors, usually twelve, who decide a verdict about the defendant—whether he is guilty or innocent. They usually meet in public in court.

7. **misdemeanor:** a minor crime, usually punishable by less than a year in jail.

8. **felony:** a serious crime, usually punishable by more than a year in prison.

9. **bail:** money paid to the court as security to ensure that the defendant will show up for his hearing or trial. If he cannot pay bail, he remains in jail awaiting trial.

## Answers to the Chart

1. crime or violation occurs
2. arrest
3. suspect not caught or not found. . .
4. booking
5. misdemeanor arraignment
6. preliminary arraignment (felony)
7. preliminary hearing
8. charges dismissed
9. grand jury
10. indictment
11. no bill
12. felony arraignment
13. trial
14. plead guilty
15. acquittal or hung jury
16. acquittal or hung jury
17. conviction
18. presentence investigation
19. sentencing

If students find this activity difficult, let them work together. Share some answers with them. (See Introduction, Hint 3, Hints for Using the Materials.)

You may wish to discuss this chart with the class. It's a gold mine! What are the implications of having so many steps in the criminal procedure? The more detailed the procedure, the more protection of one's civil liberties. Most of these steps are protected by constitutional safeguards.

Another approach might be to discuss, as fully as possible, some of these oft-quoted statements: "Justice delayed is justice denied." "Guilty beyond a reasonable doubt." "Innocent until proven guilty." Arraignments. . . . "without unnecessary delay." "Probable cause." "Excessive bail shall not be required."

# U.S.A. OUT OF CONTEXT

*All fifty states are here, in the right shape and relative size except Alaska and Hawaii, which are shown smaller than they really are. How many can you recognize by shape alone? Use a map, if you like.*

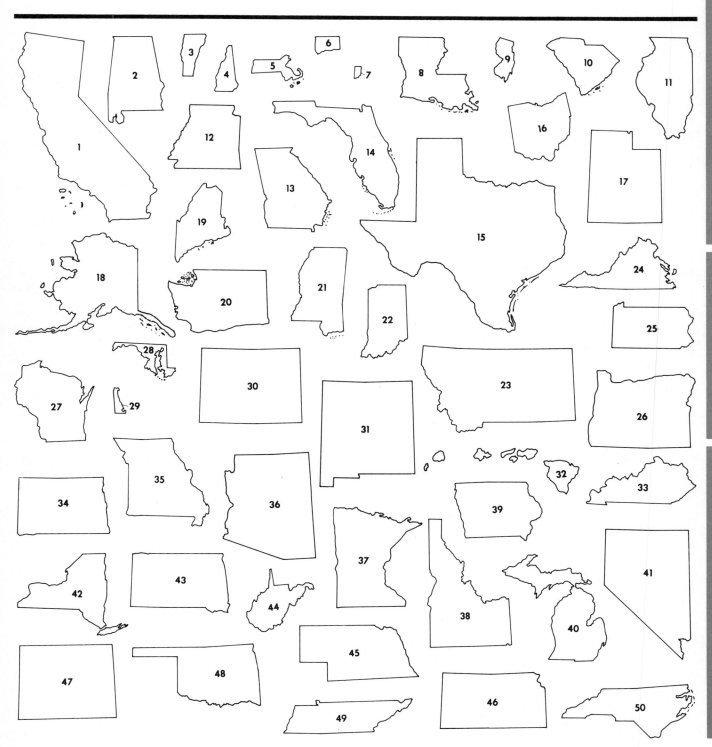

## Answers to U.S.A. Out of Context

| | | | |
|---|---|---|---|
| 1. | California | 26. | Oregon |
| 2. | Alabama | 27. | Wisconsin |
| 3. | Vermont | 28. | Maryland |
| 4. | New Hampshire | 29. | Delaware |
| 5. | Massachusetts | 30. | Colorado |
| 6. | Connecticut | 31. | New Mexico |
| 7. | Rhode Island | 32. | Hawaii |
| 8. | Louisiana | 33. | Kentucky |
| 9. | New Jersey | 34. | North Dakota |
| 10. | South Carolina | 35. | Missouri |
| 11. | Illinois | 36. | Arizona |
| 12. | Arkansas | 37. | Minnesota |
| 13. | Georgia | 38. | Idaho |
| 14. | Florida | 39. | Iowa |
| 15. | Texas | 40. | Michigan |
| 16. | Ohio | 41. | Nevada |
| 17. | Utah | 42. | New York |
| 18. | Alaska | 43. | South Dakota |
| 19. | Maine | 44. | West Virginia |
| 20. | Washington | 45. | Nebraska |
| 21. | Mississippi | 46. | Kansas |
| 22. | Indiana | 47. | Wyoming |
| 23. | Montana | 48. | Oklahoma |
| 24. | Virginia | 49. | Tennessee |
| 25. | Pennsylvania | 50. | North Carolina |

## Discussion Questions:

1. What geographical features are often natural borders between states and/or nations? *Answer:* rivers, lakes, oceans, mountains, deserts

2. From the shapes alone, can you tell which are water and which are mountain borders? *Answer:* (probably not)

3. Two types of water boundaries are distinguishable. Which are they? *Answer:* oceans and lakes, because they can have islands

4. By looking at the shapes alone (on the states on the ditto page), can you tell which have lake or ocean borders. *Answer:* There are about sixteen obvious ones.

5. Using a map of the United States, see which states have borders
   with no other states (There are two.)
   with one other state (There is one.)
   with two other states (There are four.)
   with three other states (There are eight.)
   with four other states (There are twelve.)
   with five other states (There are ten.)
   with six other states (There are nine.)
   with seven other states (There are two.)
   with eight other states (There are two.)
   Do not count water borders, like the Great Lakes.

   What do these figures tell us? In dealing with problems affecting other states, which states would have to deal with the fewest other states? the most? Can you think of circumstances in which this simple geographical fact may affect state policies and politics? (Examples that should arise might be problems involving transportation, pollution, use of natural resources such as water, drinking age limits in various states, and crime fighting.) How about your state? What are its borders like? How does your state interact with some of its neighboring states?

6. How many states border on Canada, on Mexico: *Answers:* eleven, four, respectively. Do you think it is easier to deal with another state or with another country? Think of examples involving dealings with each of these. What kinds of problems might arise at borders between nations? (examples are transportation, narcotics, payment of duties, crime fighting, pollution, and use of natural resources).

# Where am I?

**7.** Where Am I? Here are small sections of a U.S. map showing border regions of various states. Can you locate these sections and identify the states? (Copy these on the board, or use an opaque projector.)

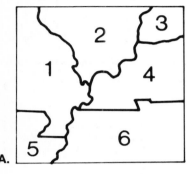
A.

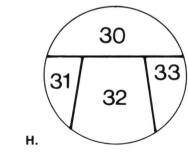
B.

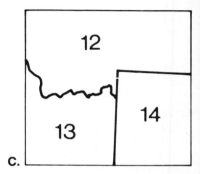
C.

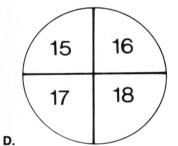
D.

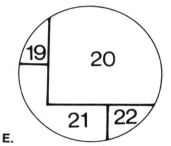
E.

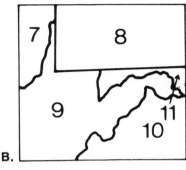
F.

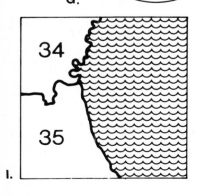
G.

H.

I.

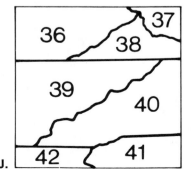
J.

K.

## Answers to Discussion Questions 4 and 5

**4.** States with obvious lake or ocean borders: Washington, New Jersey, Maine, North Carolina, Massachusetts, South Carolina, Florida, Maryland, Georgia, Louisiana, New York, Alaska, Michigan, Virginia, California, Texas. Other states with such borders: Oregon, New Hampshire, Connecticut, Rhode Island, Delaware, Alabama, Mississippi. The latter do not have large islands.

**5.** States bordering no other state: Alaska, Hawaii. States that have borders with one other state: Maine. With two state borders: Florida, Rhode Island, South Carolina, Washington. With three state borders: California, Connecticut, Delaware, Louisiana, New Hampshire, New Jersey, North Dakota, Vermont. With four state borders: Alabama, Indiana, Kansas, Maryland, Michigan, Minnesota, Mississippi, Montana, North Carolina, Oregon, Texas, Wisconsin. With five state borders: Arizona, Georgia, Illinois, Massachusetts, Nevada, New Mexico, New York, Ohio, Virginia, West Virginia. With six state borders: Arkansas, Idaho, Iowa, Nebraska, Oklahoma, Pennsylvania, South Dakota, Utah, Wyoming. With seven state borders: Colorado, Kentucky. With eight state borders: Missouri, Tennessee.

### Answers to *Where am I?*

A.  1. Missouri
    2. Illinois
    3. Indiana
    4. Kentucky
    5. Arkansas
    6. Tennessee

B.  7. Ohio
    8. Pennsylvania
    9. West Virginia
   10. Virginia
   11. Maryland

C. 12. Montana
   13. Idaho
   14. Wyoming

D. 15. Utah
   16. Colorado
   17. Arizona
   18. New Mexico

E. 19. Idaho
   20. Wyoming
   21. Utah
   22. Colorado

F. 23. California
   24. Nevada

G. 25. Colorado
   26. Kansas
   27. New Mexico
   28. Texas
   29. Oklahoma

H. 30. Tennessee
   31. Mississippi
   32. Alabama
   33. Georgia

I. 34. Georgia
   35. Florida

J. 36. Kentucky
   37. West Virginia
   38. Virginia
   39. Tennessee
   40. North Carolina
   41. Georgia
   42. Alabama

K. 43. Massachusetts
   44. Vermont
   45. New Hampshire
   46. New York
   47. Connecticut
   48. Rhode Island

# Standardized Test
# WORK/HOP

The following group of lesson ideas provides students practice in handling standardized tests without the usual tensions that build up when such tests are "for real." The lessons are useful and of interest to most students. A further advantage for the teacher is that they are very easy to prepare!

The substitute should simply bring a "how-to-study" book from a local library or bookstore for College Boards, Civil Service exams, law schools, personality tests, high school equivalency tests, and so on.

Have the students take out paper and pencil, and tell them you will read off questions from the study manual. It is best to read off about five questions at a time. Have the students answer each as best they can. Then read the answers, discuss them perhaps, and go on to the next five questions. When reading questions, skip around. For example, read about ten vocabulary questions, then ten logic questions, followed by some reading comprehension, and then back to vocabulary.

When choosing which manual to bring to class, do not feel compelled to match the exam questions to the class. A college-bound class could enjoy a Civil Service exam or a high school equivalency test, and business-bound students might enjoy the College Board exam questions. Because each group would not normally be concerned with exams out of their fields, this experience may prove to be an interesting eye-opener. Hopefully, some students will build up their confidence about tests if they find the questions easier than they had expected. Others may realize they had better get to work!

One copy of a manual, especially during the fall, winter, and early spring, will keep a high school class going for more than one period. By late spring or early summer, interest in college preparatory tests may be low, because students have already taken their exams. However, other tests, like the Civil Service or personality tests, may still be of interest.

All Subjects

Class

Other

# Substitute's BAG of
# SKILLS...TALENTS...INTERESTS...

*This series of suggestions grows out of our memory of a wonderful substitute teacher from our high school days who taught us to read the stock market pages.*

*Our present skill dates from that day when our regular teacher was out, and we were fortunate in learning something useful from a good substitute.*

As the substitute, feel free to teach whatever skills you have that might be appropriate to the class. The skills we have in mind are varied—from cooking to computers, baseball to baboons, jokes to jazz. Standard party (parlor) games such as charades, Botticelli, spelling bees, twenty questions, Simon Says (especially in foreign language classes), ghost and superghost also work well if the substitute is enthusiastic about playing them. Whatever you know, are excited about, and is appropriate, use it!

Most substitutes will be skilled in the use of at least one of these materials: stock market pages, road maps, tax tables (especially of interest in the spring!), architects' symbols, computer language, weather maps. Clever and informative lessons may be built around these. How? At the beginning of the period, you should tell what you intend to teach and why it is important. This might be discussed with the class. Enthusiasm will be important in helping convince the class that the topic is of interest to them.

To run the lesson efficiently, you should have enough copies of the chart, map, or whatever for groups of two's or three's to share, or one copy may be shown on an opaque projector. Use whichever method is more convenient.

One way to start is by explaining a few of the basic symbols. You might write them on the board. Be sure all students understand them. Then ask some questions to test their use of the symbols. Continue to explain more symbols, a few at a time, until all are understood. Keep the lesson logical, in a step-by-step progression. Another way to proceed is to ask the class to tell you what they think the symbols mean. This is closer to the inquiry method of teaching. Build the system of symbols on the class's thinking and insights.

Next, make up problems and questions and puzzles using whatever knowledge or skill is being taught and learned. If you are not sure you can do this spontaneously, it is best to work out these questions ahead of time. After a few such lessons, the whole process will probably become comfortable and quite automatic.

After a few of your questions, you may ask the class to make up some. This process may become competitive, by having one student or group start and having whoever answered the questions continue by asking one of his own. By the end of the period, the class should be confident with the new skill and feel satisfied that they have learned something new and potentially useful.

All Subjects · English · Foreign Language · Math · Science · Social Science

Class · Groups · Individuals

Dittos · Dittos* · Blackboard · Other · Quickie